Things I
Noticed About

LOST

Past Perceptions
& Future Theories

by Vozzek

©2009 Daniel McAleese

Printed by: Maven Master Inc.
199 lee ave suite 611
Brooklyn, NY 11211

Library of Congress Cataloging-in-Publication Pending
McAleese, Daniel A.
Things You Never Noticed About LOST
Past Perceptions & Future Theories / by Vozzek

ISBN-13: 978-0-9843556-0-0
1. Lost (Television Program) I. Title.

Special thanks to Andy, Anil, Karen, and Erika for the
support and encouragement necessary to complete this book.

Extra special thanks to every answer-starved fan out there
who has helped make LOST *way* more than just your
average network television show about
monsters eating people in a jungle.

• Printed and bound in the United States of America •

Cntents

Introduction

"Dude, are you watching LOST? You *have* to be watching that show, no?"

These were my cousin Eddie's words to me in late 2004. It was almost Christmas, and we stood side by side during hockey warm-up, shooting balls into a open net. Between slapshots, we had what amounted to a forty-second conversation. Looking back at it now though, that forty seconds would account for an *awful* lot of my future time.

"Isn't that the show with the plane crash?", I asked him.

"No man, it's more than that!" Eddie stopped shooting balls for a moment and leaned on his stick. "There's a monster that eats people, and there's this hatch in the jungle..."

"A monster that eats people?", I interrupted him. I didn't know if his description was supposed to help get me excited about the show, but it was having an opposite effect.

"Yeah, but you don't see it. They never show the monster. But the hatch! I *gotta* know what's in that damned hatch!"

I'd never seen Eddie this excited over anything but football, much less a TV show, much less a *drama* that was on major network television. The whole thing just wasn't Eddie's style.

"What hatc-" I began to ask him... but at that exact moment a referee's whistle marked the beginning of our bitterly cold, bottom-division hockey game.

"It's out of CONTROL, dude", my cousin told me, taking his position at right wing. "You gotta watch it. Trust me."

Several weeks passed, and winter gave way to spring without me having seen a single episode of LOST. It's not that I didn't trust Eddie, it was more that I didn't want to start watching a show from the middle of the season. I did file it away in the back of my mind though, to keep an eye out for it if I could ever catch it from the beginning.

Spring turned into summer, and I finally caught a promo for LOST's pilot as the network was about to re-run the whole season. Grabbing my remote, I set the DVR to record it when it came on. A few days later there it was, staring back at me from my long list of things I wished I had the time to watch. But remembering how excited Eddie seemed to be about the show, I leaned back on the couch and pressed the play button.

As they say, the rest is history.

Like most of you reading this book right now, the Pilot episode of LOST totally blew me away. When *Tabula Rasa* aired the next week, I watched it live. By the time John Locke wiggled his toes in *Walkabout*, I was completely hooked. Eddie was right. This show *was* out of control. I watched it religiously week after week, going bananas when Locke and Boone first stumbled across the hatch. Somewhere in the middle of the run, I realized the season one DVD's had come out. Twenty minutes later I was popping them into my disc player, and I think I watched the whole rest of the season within a day of owning them.

By the time the credits rolled on *Exodus Part 2*, I had the phone in my hand. My cousin was of little help - he had even less of a clue what was in the hatch than I did. My next stop was of course the internet, which eventually lead me to imdb.com, which put me right smack in the middle of a very heated LOST forum. Months after the initial airing of the season one finale, there were still dozens of threads being created each day as people speculated about the contents of the hatch. Just like Eddie and I, everyone else was dying to know what the hell was in there.

The people on the imdb message boards weren't just passionate about the show, they were borderline ferocious. Debates raged about everything from Purgatory to Armageddon. There were threads about the numbers, the flashbacks, why Hurley wasn't losing any weight and how the characters managed to wipe their asses without any toilet paper. And when it came to the hatch, the opinions were overwhelming. Some thought the whisperers lived down there, while others thought it was the nanobot laboratory responsible for the creation of the smoke monster. Those enrolled in the school of rational thought pinned it as an entrance to The Others' hideout, while the sci-fi fans touted it as a portal to another world or dimension. There was even one guy who was convinced there was a whole subway train down there, with tracks that ran to and from God knows where. In fact, he was so sure of his opinion that he posted it daily, challenged everyone who disagreed with him, and vowed to come back the night of the season two premiere to flaunt it in everyone's face. A day before the episode aired however, spoilers revealed what was *really* in the hatch... and as you can imagine we never saw that guy's screen name again.

I dove headfirst into the imdb message boards and quickly became one of those rabid LOST fans. I chose the screen name 'Vozzek', but when I found out it was taken I appended my hockey jersey's number to it: 69. This wasn't a tribute to my cousin or anything symbolic, I was just in a hurry to log on and post my opinions. Of course I had no better clue than anyone else when it came to what was going on, but I sure loved to speculate about it. Very quickly I found out that talking about LOST with people who love the show - even ferociously - was almost as much fun as actually watching it.

Experiencing season two alongside my imdb friends was a great way to watch the show. As it became clear we were seeing much more than a TV drama about a plane crash, people really started getting involved with the imagery and metaphors of LOST. The scenes weren't just something you watched and moved on from - you drank them in, and started to wonder if there were alternate ways to interpret them. New mysteries spawned new debates. The day after each episode aired there were plenty of threads talking about what happened the night before, but the ones that were most interesting to me were always the conversations that theorized about what it all *meant*. Speculating about what was going to happen in future episodes became one of my favorite things to post about.

Admittedly, some of my theories were pretty far out there. Then again, so was the show. For a while there were a lot people clinging to the belief that everything on LOST would be scientifically explained, and that all of its mysteries would turn out to be based in science fact, not fiction. These posters liked to fight with me, shooting down my assertions that the island had an agenda of its own, or that the very thoughts and needs of LOST's characters were being subconsciously manifested through the power of their own suggestions. I took a lot of heat for a while, and there were cyber-mobs with torches out to lynch me. In the end though, it was a hell of a lot of fun. Even the flame wars were cool, because disagreeing with someone so vehemently could often bring out theories and ideas - on both sides of the argument - that no one had ever really thought of before.

In the second week of season three, I created a post called "Things I Noticed About the Glass Ballerina." For the most part it was a bunch of sarcastic observations that I was just having fun with. At the time, one of the more regular posters on the forum was a guy going by the name of DarkUFO. In an instant message to me, he explained that he'd started a LOST website and asked if he could copy my post over there for his viewers to read. I told him to go for it, and it generated enough positive response that he asked for my thoughts on the next week's episode too. Without really wanting or realizing it, this turned into a regular thing, with me sending over my thoughts and Dark appending "Things I Noticed" onto the front of every episode title.

Since then Andy Page, owner of *darkufo.blogspot.com*, has become a pretty good friend of mine. I've been asked to do interviews, make guest posts, and record audio podcasts with TheODI. I've even had a fan come to my house once to watch LOST with me (and I made her bring popcorn). But best of all I've made some really great friends from all over the world - friends who I'll still have long after the curtain finally closes on the series finale. And incredibly, all this because of one little TV show that I almost didn't even watch.

In the immortal words of eight paragraphs ago, the rest is history. I've put forth dozens of theories and hundreds of personal observations on LOST over the past three years. Since the beginning, I've never been afraid to speak my mind on exactly what I believe is going on and what I think is going to happen next. At times, this has pissed some people off. There are readers who have stumbled across my column expecting to read a more traditional "recap" (I always hated that word) of each episode, and they seem to get offended when they're served up a steaming hot dish of my own opinions. Then there are others; those who think I've gotten more and more theory-orientated as time goes on. Is this true? Of course it is. Because for the first time since LOST began, we finally have more answers than questions. Forming theories is getting easier and easier, and the theories themselves that people come up with seem to be zeroing in a lot closer to the mark.

I've never made apologies for the Things *I've* Noticed. In voicing my opinions on the show I've been both gloriously right and cataclysmically wrong. I've hit the nail right on the head about some things... and other times I've been way, wayyyy off. But through it all, I think I've always been welcoming of other people's ideas. Some of the best talks about LOST are spawned through disagreement, and the duality of the show even reflects this doctrine. Science vs. Faith, Free Will vs. Fate, and most recently, Everything Changes vs. Whatever Happened, Happened. In five great seasons LOST has developed a strong cult of followers, all of varying opinion, each of us trying to figure out the exact same thing: just how the hell is it all going to end?

In writing this book, I want you all to know that I didn't skimp out on you. Just as my columns weren't traditional episode recaps, this book isn't going to give you a five-season play by play of what happened on LOST so far. "Kate did this... and then Jack said that... and then Locke came along and threw a knife at someone." Too many LOST books already do that, and there's too little time left. If you're a fan of the show, you should *know* what happened so far - after all, you're the one sitting there watching it. Hopefully, you bought this book to help figure out *why* it happened. You're reading it to get some fresh ideas, temper them with your own thoughts, and in the end, hammer out some ultimate meaning in the grand scheme of the LOST universe.

This book you're holding contains the latest and greatest thoughts, observations, and theories on LOST after five whole seasons of the show. Some of these theories are my own, a few of them are grounded elsewhere, and still others are commonly accepted ideas that I've expanded upon because they've evolved greatly since their inception. In all cases, I've worked hard to give specific evidence to support them - even the ones I don't agree with. Some of them I absolutely love, others I'm not so crazy about... but in the end they're all here for you to make your own decisions regarding what's going to happen - or not happen - by the end of next season.

I always promised myself that if I ever wrote a book, I wouldn't include some lame, boring intro. Hopefully I didn't. As Johnny Locke would say, let's get moving...

Vozzek
Summer, 2009

LOST Five Years Later... Where Are We?

The island. For five seasons we've tried to unlock its mysteries, and for five seasons new ones keep springing back up in their place. But if there's one thing we've learned in more than a hundred episodes, it's that within the LOST universe, the island is not just a place - it's also a living, breathing character of its own.

So just what is the island? Will we ever find out? I'm pretty sure that final mystery will be left unsolved by the time the show ends. Oh, I think we're going to get a lot of good answers... but we'll never get the end-all, be-all solution to that one big question. For six seasons we'll have watched anything and everything occur on the island, but the final answer as to exactly what the island is? That will probably be left open to interpretation.

That being said, I'm sure we can all agree on one thing: it's not *just* an island. It's a shape-shifting, ever-changing limbo in which our main characters are somehow caught. The island has needs and wants. It has laws and rules. The island bestows incredible gifts and just as quickly takes them back. It guides its inhabitants along the path to do its bidding, and punishes them severely when they stray. And if you believe the smoke monster is part of the island itself? It also judges people - tests them - and destroys whomever it deems unworthy.

Writing down everything we know about the island sure doesn't help. It's in the middle of the Pacific Ocean... sometimes. It's got unusual magnetic properties. It's got extraordinary healing capabilities. It's a tropical paradise filled with ancient ruins, crashed planes, broken ships, and the occasional polar bear. And let's not even talk about the magic box.

Applying logic or science to the island doesn't work either: it's a mystical place, with magical properties. It's a big sticky ball rolling through time and space, picking up whatever people and objects happen to be in its path along the way. You can't define the island any more than you can define how it works, which is why anyone watching LOST needs to keep one thing in mind: *nothing* should be taken at face value.

And if you're like me? At this point you're doubting whether there's even an island at all. I mean sure, it's there. It's the first thing Jack sees when he opens his eyes. But as the final season of LOST draws to a close, I suspect the difference between what Jack sees, what Kate sees, and what Vincent the yellow dog sees will be radically different from what *actually is*. Much more on that in the Theory section.

THE GAME BOARD

For now though, it's safe to say that the island is the giant game board upon which LOST is played, and our characters are little more than the pieces scattered across it. We could be watching backgammon, chess, or even Mouse Trap - it doesn't really matter what you call it. What matters is that just like any game, the board has boundaries and limitations. The pieces each have their own available set of legal moves. And the players? Well, they're bound by the overall rules of the game. Whether they choose to play strictly by the rules or bend them a bit, that's an entirely different story.

And hey, maybe you don't like the game analogy at all. In that case, think of LOST as a big, multi-part play. The island is the stage and the characters the actors, with each season consisting of its own separate act. One by one everyone plays their part, each of them there "for a reason." Some roles are killed off early on in the story while others stick around for a while, integral to the final resolution of the plot.

Even the set design changes from act to act, from the mysterious jungles of season one to the Swan hatch of season two. Season three was dominated by The Other's encampments, and in season four we even got a glimpse into the off-island real world... or so we're lead to believe. And season five? That set changed like the bouncing ball of a giant roulette wheel, before finally coming to rest on 1970's Dharma.

The playing field of the island is as dynamic as its many characters, places, and themes. In some ways it's even too dynamic... its many coincidences a little too convenient. A heroin addict finding a planeload of heroin... a man finding his lost brother half a world away. As the coincidences get piled on top of even wilder coincidences, the island itself is even called into question. And when the characters begin popping impossibly in and out of each other's flashbacks? Well, let's just say if you believe that the beeping of the Swan's doomsday clock just *happened* to sound like the timer from Desmond's microwave, the rest of this book may not be for you.

Because very simply put, consider this: if the flashbacks are suspect, everything that happens on the show should be questioned. As cutout ladybug and butterfly pictures jump from the walls of Santa Rosa's mental ward in *The Beginning of the End* all the way to Kate's refrigerator during *Something Nice Back Home*, even what we take for granted as "the real world" may not be so real after all.

So where does the reality of the island end and the fantasy world begin? At what point are we looking at something real, or something imagined? Somewhere on the stage of LOST is a great big curtain, and everything just beyond the view of that curtain may not be part of the show. As the same stage props get dragged out again and again, we're left to wonder how many times before this story has played out... and as Jacob and his dark-shirted friend would argue, whether or not it always ends the same way.

And besides ourselves, does the island perhaps have another

audience? A hidden congregation of onlookers watching everything that happens? The whispers we hear in the jungle, the glimpses of people and things that just don't seem to belong - these things flash quickly away before we get a chance to fully realize them. Are these members of a whole different group of spectators, one that's already been removed from the island's stage or playing field? In the words of Cindy the flight attendant, maybe there are people in the story who, like us, are just "here to watch."

When it comes to picking a stage upon which to tell a six-year long story, the jungles of LOST couldn't have been a better choice. From watching flashbacks to flash-forwards to even traveling through time, we've been able to see the past, present and future of the island through the eyes of those who've experienced its very possessive shores. And unless its true nature is finally revealed, it's very likely that the island's biggest mysteries will continue to live on long after the story of LOST has ended.

THE PIECES

Upon the giant game board of LOST are the playing pieces, or in this case, the characters of the story. Season by season these people are revealed to us, from the main group of survivors of Oceanic Flight 815 to the tail section characters of season two. Also residing on the island are The Others - a group of natives kept by the island to help maintain its own interests. Most of them are nonessential, but some - like Ben, Richard, and Juliet - end up becoming major pieces in the overall game itself.

Like most other games these pieces are removed from the board as they're captured or killed, but unlike most games new pieces are constantly being added to keep things interesting. In season five we learn that Jacob's himself, a man who just might be one of the main players, is responsible for bringing in these new characters, and therefore constantly changing the dynamic of the game. Turns out he's been doing this for what could be hundreds of years now, and for just as long the man in the dark shirt has been working to counter his every move.

Desmond, Rousseau, the Black Rock, the freighter crew - all of these pieces have been marched across the island's game board at one time or another, seemingly brought there for a purpose. As they succeed or fail at whatever it is they're supposed to accomplish, we're repeatedly given evidence that none of them seem to have a will of their own. We the viewers and even the characters themselves are led to believe that their destiny is set in stone: their fate sealed the moment the island grabbed hold of them. None of what they do really matters, as everything is predetermined from the very beginning. This polishes the razor-sharp edges of what soon become LOST's biggest recurring themes: science vs. faith, free will vs. destiny.

Now of course we knew none of this stuff when the show first started. In season one we were just watching a really cool plane crash and the interesting character conflicts that arose from 48 people trying to live together on a deserted island. Back then everyone controlled their own actions - or so we thought - with maybe the exception of John Locke, the first person to receive the island's guidance. But as the seasons wore on, the delicate balance between fate and free will became the very crux of the show. We realized this right alongside the main characters... and as soon as they did, they chose up sides. Some of them even found themselves flip-flopping from one side to the other, depending upon what happened to them as they went along.

And through everything we've got other important elements of the show: redemption, closure, and resolution of inner conflict. The characters of LOST struggle to accept on-island solutions to their off-island problems, growing and changing in the process. They're shown strange visions, walking corpses, and monsters that tear trees out by the roots. Some of them are able to accept these things for what they are, and this makes up the group that embraces faith. Others cling more tightly to logic and reality, and are slapped with the label of science.

Yet even more important to us (and them) is the overall bigger question: who's playing this game? For five seasons our heroes have been trying to get to the bottom of that issue, and just as we think we're getting some good answers another level of authority is revealed. Layer by layer the onion has been peeled back to show us that even the higher ups like Ben and Richard don't have a clue as to what's going on; even they are only operating on the belief that they're following some higher order of good. It took all the way until the end of season five to finally meet the all-important Jacob, only to watch him die... leaving us all wondering if maybe there's not someone above even him that must be running the show.

Still, the variety and range of characters on LOST has kept the show fun, funny, and exciting all at the same time. Even better, the roles each character ends up playing might change from one season to the next, adding yet another spin to an already great story. In the span of five seasons we've seen Jack go from the group's self-appointed leader and doctor all the way down to a Dharma janitor that refuses to give medical attention. On the flip side of that same coin, Sawyer's transformation has him going from a selfish, materialistic convict all the way up to a caring, self-sacrificing, chief of security. John Locke's assertion that "everyone's here for a reason" might well be right, but with character roles constantly changing, it's hard to know what those reasons will be until the very end of the show.

THE PLAYERS

All throughout LOST we've seen game analogies too numerous to list. We've watched the characters playing these various games, but over time we've come to realize that they themselves might be part of a much bigger power struggle. Finding out just what this game is, and which two sides are playing it, has been the show's biggest and most long-standing mystery.

And who's to say there are only two sides? As Mikhail points out the computerized chess game to Locke in *Enter 77*, he makes mention of "three grand masters." He also notifies Locke that the game cheats, a sentiment echoed by Benjamin Linus as he accuses Charles Widmore of doing just that. The dark-shirted man might argue that a loophole isn't really a cheat at all, which is how he makes his ultimate play on Jacob during the season five finale. If Richard Alpert's Book of Laws is proven to be the rulebook of LOST's big game, it seems there are definite ways around these rules for those who look for them.

Season after season, LOST teases us with finding out the identity of the man behind the curtain, even creating an episode with that exact title. As we starved for answers, we all knew the real meat and potatoes of what was going on lay with the puppetmaster or masters. They'd be the only ones who could answer that one huge question for us: *why*. Why were all these things happening, over and over again, in never-ending loops that always seemed destined to fold over on each other? Getting hold of the man in charge became top priority for us, blowing away all other questions about the smoke monster, the numbers, or why the toilet in the Pearl hatch somehow still works.

For five years we've marched up the island's chain of command, seeking to know the truth. Ben, Widmore, Richard, and now Jacob... each time we're sure we're getting to the top it seems there might be just one more person that needs to be answered to. Even as seasons six looms before us, no one can be sure that we've reached the summit just yet. Learning that there's someone or something that even Jacob reports to shouldn't surprise us one bit, but ultimately LOST will have to pull back the curtain the rest of the way... and finally show us who's *really* playing the game.

As Locke Tells Walt in the Pilot episode: "Two players. Two sides. One is light, one is dark." This certainly points a finger at Jacob and his nemesis, wearing light and dark shirts during the opening scene of *The Incident*. So are these the players? With what looks to be the Black Rock approaching in the distance, Jacob seems to be bringing his own chess pieces to the island's game board. He's ready to manipulate and move them around, just as his opponent is ready to counter them with moves of his own. Are these the two sides we've heard so much about? Is this "the war" Charles Widmore keeps referring to, the one he's so concerned that the right side should win?

You'd tend to think so. And yet there's an even higher level of game-playing going on here, one we find out about by the end of the episode. The stakes of the game between Jacob and his nemesis seem to be life and death itself. As the dark-shirted man completes his long con, it seems like he's finally put his opponent into checkmate. But does Jacob still have a play? A loophole, or long con of his own? By flashing back through the main characters' past lives and touching each one of them, has he provided himself an out?

And above all else, what do Jacob's final words, "They're coming", mean? The game can't be over just yet - we've still got an entire season left to go. It seemed a warning to his nemesis more than anything else, which is why it seems so fascinating. It makes me think we'll see someone even higher up on the food chain than either of these two characters. Someone so important that their arrival would worry both Jacob *and* his opponent. For a moment, imagine the two of them as children playing some forbidden game, hearing the footsteps of their approaching parents. The whole idea of that just gives me the shivers.

THE END GAME

Anyone who's watched LOST all this time has developed certain theories about one thing or another. This is because the show not only challenges you to figure out what's going on, but what's *really* happening. There are some straightforward episodes that can be taken at face value, but even during those you can find subtle hits and important nods toward solving certain mysteries of the island. And in five seasons, we've seen an overwhelming amount of fantastic, inexplicable things that have always left us wondering.

But examining the biggest question of all: Just how does LOST end?

With the regular season finales containing some of the biggest plot twists in the whole show, should we expect LOST to end with a twist? Will those big white letters slam into our TV screens while our jaws are still touching the floor? Probably not. But I do think we've got one last twist in store for us, and it's probably going to be the biggest one yet. If I had to guess, I'd say we'll see that twist somewhere around the last two or three episodes. This would give the writers time to resolve things, tie up loose ends, and to conclude each character's storyline in a way that satisfies most of the viewers.

The producers claim to have conceived LOST's ending before even a single episode aired, and I tend to believe them. Even so, constructing that ending in such a way to satisfy the show's hungry fans has got to be an imposing task. It's obvious by now that no ending will make *everyone* happy, but if LOST's conclusion is even half as mind-blowing as it could be? It should be legendary. Regardless of how popular the show has become or what type of audience is now watching, I hope the creators stick to their initial concept no matter how crazy it might be. As executive producers Damon Lindelof and Carlton Cuse said during Comic Con 09', "trust us."

But there's a question even bigger than how LOST ends, and that's whether or not there's an overall "answer" to everything. The island has big mysteries and small ones, and by the time it's over we're going to get most of our juicier questions answered. But is there a *big* answer? Is there one giant solution to what's going on with the island and what's happening to these characters? Sure we may find out what happens, but will we ever find out *why*?

I tend to think so.

I'm reminded of an episode of *The Twilight Zone*, called "Five Characters in Search of an Exit." Five people wake up in a circular room with high walls open to the sky. They're all very different: a soldier, a clown, a ballerina, a hobo, a bagpiper... none of them remember who they are, or how they got there. A strange bell keeps ringing above them, so loudly that they cover their ears and cringe. They theorize that they're dead, or that they're in Limbo. They wonder if they're really there at all, or if everything they see is an illusion. Someone suggests that maybe they're all dreaming, and each of them is part of the other person's dream. "Where are we?", the soldier screams. "What are we? Who are we?" Interestingly, these are all questions our LOST characters have asked at one time or another. These are all things we've wondered since the beginning of the show.

Eventually, the camera pans out to reveal the true answer: the circular room is a metal collection bin. The characters are all dolls, unwanted toys left for charity. The bell belongs to a Salvation Army worker, ringing it to attract attention during the holiday season.

Will the ending of LOST be this literal? This final? Probably not. The writers are going to end the show with plenty of mysteries left open to interpretation. Still, I can't help but feel there's an overall answer to Charlie's question of

"Where are we?" And when Jack grabs hold of Achara and shakes her, demanding "Tell me who I am!", I'm of the opinion that we're going to find out *exactly* who Jack really is... and when we do, that the answer might blow everyone's head apart.

THE THEORIES

As a LOST fan, some of the most fun you'll have is theorizing about what's up next. Whether you're a casual viewer or you dig a little deeper into the show, you can literally spend hours talking about what happened after an episode, and what it means for the future. And for people like me? Putting together my own theories and listening to other peoples' ideas on LOST is almost as much fun as actually watching the show. Without theories, you wouldn't be holding this book.

Are the main characters dead? Are they in Purgatory? Is the island a big alien space ship? Since season one people have been trying to unlock LOST's bigger mysteries by examining the evidence and trying to look through the big curtain. As diehard fans we've all counted instances of the numbers, rearranged letters to form anagrams, even played audio clips backwards in order to try and figure out what's going on. Sometimes we're rewarded with actual clues, and other times the writers are just having fun with us. Knowing when we're being shown something important and when we're being bamboozled isn't always easy, especially as the clues get bigger and the answers come faster as they have in later seasons.

If you've read anything I've ever written, you know I love to theorize. Although my writings are characterized as 'recaps', I've never considered myself a recapper of the show. I've always enjoyed going out on a limb, not just summarizing plot lines for each episode, but actually examining *why* things happened and trying to predict what's going to happen next. In doing so, I've come up with a lot of crazy theories over the last few years. Some of them proved to be spot on, while others turned out to be totally wrong. Either way, I put them out there for everyone to see, week after week, good or bad. And for the most part, the response has been favorable.

I think that's because for every one person who's somehow offended by incorrect assumptions and insights, there are ten other people who just love to speculate. Anyone can factually rehash an episode of LOST for you. Anyone can give you a paragraph by paragraph summary of what happened last night, and they can proudly be 100% accurate. But those who put their own ideas out there - at the risk of getting them squashed - are the ones who can really get you thinking. It's fun to imagine what the island's true agenda actually is, or who's running the show. The LOST fan community consists of some highly creative people, and we all love to look ahead and picture how things are going to finally turn out - especially with the show's final season just on the horizon.

In short, theorizing is fun. Which is why everything I've

ever written has been geared toward trying to hammer out answers to the show's bigger questions. In past seasons, this was tough. We had some tremendous mysteries and very little to go on. But now, after 100+ episodes, there's a lot more evidence to examine. When considering how things will finally play out, we've got more than enough to go on. Has someone hit on the big answer yet? Who knows? But with an ever-increasing amount of clues and evidence, everyone's theories keep getting better and better.

Beyond this page you'll read some of the coolest, wildest, and most outlandish ideas about what's going on in LOST. Some are old, and some are new. A few of these theories are my own, and the rest are my thoughts on some of the better concepts floating around out there. Although you'll read evidence to back these theories up, understand that none of them are foolproof. Whether you agree or disagree with them isn't so important as gathering *your own* thoughts and ideas while you read them.

Is there a single theory out there that can explain everything? Probably not. For that reason you should approach these concepts like a chef, taking ingredients that you like from each of them and creating your own unique recipe for what you think is happening. That's the fun of LOST. The show might end when the credits roll, but you can spend the rest of the week deciding what you just saw.

Suggestive Manifestation

"I saw it! I actually saw it in my mind, like it was real or something!"
- Walt, *Special*

"Two days after I found out I had a fatal tumor on my spine, a spinal surgeon fell out of the sky..."
- Benjamin Linus, *The Cost of Living*

"It was only as real as you made it."
- John Locke, *Hearts & Minds*

"Guess that falls under the category of be careful what you wish for."
- Kate, *Hearts & Minds*

Suggestive manifestation isn't so much a theory as it is a concept used to explain some of the more bizarre coincidences within LOST. It can be applied all the way back to the opening episodes of season one, when anything and everything the main characters wanted seemed to appear out of thin air whenever they needed it to. Way back then however, LOST hadn't gone overly supernatural. No one wanted to believe that the island was magically providing these things, and a good many viewers blasted the theory as nonsense. They wanted rational explanations for everything, even the smoke monster. These were the original men and women of science, and they didn't even know it yet.

From the very beginning, things began popping up whenever desired, imagined, feared, or thought about - even subconsciously. From Jack's dead father walking the beach to Charlie stumbling across a planeload of heroin, it became obvious that the island was manifesting these things through the character's own thoughts or memories. Even John Locke gets up and walks away from the plane crash on two good legs... a gift from the island, no doubt. But how does he throw knives with deadly accuracy? Do you think he learned to hunt, track, slaughter, and skin boars just from shooting birds with his dad? Or did he acquire these great skills back at his job stocking shelves at Toys R' Us?

Knowing what we know about him now in season five, John Locke just might be a special exemption. Let's look at Kate's black stallion... or Sawyer's boar. One manifested by Kate's constant desire to run, the other created by Sawyer's nagging guilt over having killed an innocent man. In *White Rabbit*, Jack goes into the jungle to find water and shelter, and stumbles across both with his discovery of the caves. "How did you find this place?", Kate asks him. "Luck", Jack tells her.

Claire thinks her baby might get sick, and so it does. Hurley's having a tough time dealing with food and suddenly Dave shows up, easily plucked from his subconscious and manifested by the island. And consider this for a moment: What if the numbers keep appearing because Hurley keeps obsessing over them, and not the other way around? What if the numbers are there *because* of Hurley, instead of Hurley being there because of the numbers?

And let's take Mr. Eko. He hears of a crashed plane on the island, and he wants very badly for it to be his brother's missing Beechcraft. So badly that it actually *becomes* his brother's missing plane. Wild coincidence? No. Self-fulfilling prophecy, courtesy of the island. And hey, didn't Eko's memories get scanned by the smoke monster right before they found the plane? You bet they did.

Even Sayid falls victim to his own greatest fears, in which he's forced to perform the same questionable things he had to do in the Iraqi Republican Guard. The island won't let him escape his past as a torturer. Instead, the guilt and remorse he's constantly plagued with over his past deeds are manifested into reality: Sayid is once again forced to use these skills. Like the phantom boar Sawyer conjures up with his own regret, this isn't something Sayid wanted, but something that he created nonetheless.

Going even one step further, finding things has always been easy for the survivors of Flight 815. Do you think Kate and

Sawyer just happened to stumble across the Marshal's Haliburton case in *Whatever the Case May Be*? Or do you think Kate found it because she wanted what was inside so very badly? And if you strike that one up as coincidence, consider Nikki and Paulo. Desperate to find their stolen diamonds, they happen to find their own bag in exactly the same spot, in exactly the same lake. The odds on that are not too shabby.

Locke the hunter also manages to find his own piece of luggage, filled with exactly what he needs right now: a long row of razor-sharp knives. But in Locke's case you have to wonder: did he really pack that suitcase at all? Was it a gift from the island... was it there because he *wanted* it to be there? Even though he was going on a walkabout, the answer is suspect. As Charlie says in *White Rabbit*, "Who packs 400 knives?"

The island bestowing such gifts on its inhabitants is nothing new. Call it accelerated healing or the island's will - the use of Locke's legs was restored to him so he could do its bidding. Apparently it trades for things as well. When Charlie wishes he had his guitar, Locke assures him it will turn up. He's also the first to understand the island's need for judgment and sacrifice, telling Charlie "The island will give you your guitar back, but first you have to give the island something." Charlie hands over his heroin, and Locke points upward... to show Charlie's guitar lodged in some jungle vines, perfectly intact despite having survived a two thousand-foot fall from the sky.

Miraculous as the island's power may be, nothing compares to the apparent manifestation powers of Walt. The appearance of a polar bear on the island was a pretty big mystery, until you consider the polar bear in Walt's comic book. We see Walt do things on the island that no other character can do. In *Tabula Rasa*, Michael tells Walt "I'm gonna find your dog as soon as it stops raining." Walt looks up at the rain, it instantly stops, and then he looks pointedly back at his father. These types of abilities are what makes Walt very interesting to The Others, so important and desirable that they pluck him from the rescue raft at the end of season one.

Yet Walt's abilities spill over into his flashbacks too, and that might be what makes him so special. From the moment the bird from Walt's book crashes into his window, we realize that he can make things happen off-island as well. We're led to believe that he has a gift, and the Others get "more than they bargained for" when they seize Walt to examine that gift. He demonstrates the ability to project himself beyond his captivity, causing The Others to lock him in Room 23 as they attempt to control his talents. The very fact that Ben lets him leave the island at the end of season two seems to indicate Walt is simply too dangerous to be kept around.

But is Walt really the only person that's gifted? Later on in season three we see Juliet's ex-husband get creamed by a bus, not long after Juliet had wished he'd be hit by one. As in Walt's situation, this happens off the island - within a flashback - and Richard Alpert goes on to tell Juliet that she's special. In fact, the list of people who've been called "special" is pretty long. Ms. Hawking tells her son Daniel that he's special. Both Charlie and Locke's mothers say the same thing about them. Ben was told he was special as a child, and Hurley is told he's special because he can see Jacob's cabin. Desmond is even referred to as "uniquely and miraculously special."

So is there anyone who's *not* special on the island? Is everything just a figment of someone else's imagination, subconsciously made concrete through the island's doing?

Later on we're shown evidence that the polar bears were leftover subjects from Dharma's zoology experiments, seeming to shatter the theory that Walt or Hurley somehow conjured them up by reading that comic book. But what would you say if I told you there were no such experiments? What if I suggested that the Dharma zoology program was nothing more than a hoax perpetuated by The Others - from the cages Kate and Sawyer sat in all the way down to Mr. Friendly's mention of bears - just to keep the 815 survivors from knowing the truth?

After all, can polar bears adapt to live in the tropics? Did they swim from the smaller island to the main one? Is it so far fetched to think that Ben and his followers, already putting on costumes and fake beards to fool the main characters, wouldn't go a few steps further to keep them in the dark? How much of the island is real, and what portions of it are props or stages made to look like something else in order to hide the truth?

The Magic Box

Answers to those questions are hard to come by, especially considering how often lies get told in the story of LOST. I was nearly lynched on the imdb message boards for suggesting the island was manifesting these things, at least until *The Man From Tallahassee* finally aired. That's when Ben spilled a few juicy beans to Locke, explaining the inner workings of the island to him: "What if I told you that somewhere on this island there's a very large box... and whatever you imagined... whatever you wanted to be in it... when you opened that box, there it would be."

Taking Ben's words as fact, it would explain a great many things. As he later says, the box is only a metaphor. There's nothing specific about where or when the island manifests these things, only that other people are indirectly responsible for bringing them into existence. When Ben tells Richard to bring the "man from Tallahassee", it's because that's how they first knew him when they found him - on island. It probably took Ben a little while to find out who Anthony Cooper was before attributing his arrival on the island, via the magic box, to John Locke.

In truth however, Cooper's arrival on the island probably has more to do with Sawyer wanting so badly to find the con man responsible for the death of his parents. Not even Ben realizes this, which is why when Locke questions his arrival, Ben shrugs him off with "You tell me. You brought him here."

Later on, Ben demands that Locke deal with Anthony Cooper, telling him "It's your mess John, you clean it up." And for some reason, the same John Locke who throws a knife into Naomi's back in *Through the Looking Glass* just can't bring himself to kill a man who stole his kidney and tried to murder him. Instead, he gets Sawyer to do it. Which makes you wonder if the person who activates the box must be the one who deals with whatever he or she brought through it... Sawyer dealing with Cooper, Hurley dealing with Dave, Eko dealing with Yemi... the list could go on and on.

But now consider this: if the magic box is creating or manifesting whatever people can imagine, who on the island has the most vivid imagination of all? Who would have the most innocently creative thoughts, dreams, and fears with which to bring all sorts of crazy possibilities unknowingly into existence?

The answer to that question is startlingly simple: the children. This may be why The Others were so quick to abduct the youngest members of the Flight 815 crash survivors. Zach, Emma, and eventually Walt - these were the young minds, the wild, dangerously imaginative brains that could inadvertently create havoc if left unchecked. Children believe in all sorts of fantastic things, from superheroes to monsters. Who knows what they could conjure up without even realizing it?

The children were good and they were innocent, and they were taken to a "better place" for those reasons too. But if suggestive manifestation is responsible for the creation of what could potentially be unlimited danger? Pulling them from LOST's stage as quickly as possible makes a whole lot of sense. Ditto for keeping the Flight 815 survivors in the dark about the inner workings of the island, many of them having already unknowingly created dopplegangers of their own.

I use the phrase doppleganger here, because to call these creations real people would be a gross misconception. The line between what's real and what's imaginary becomes very blurred on the island, especially as the seasons wear on. Suffice it to say Richard certainly didn't sail to Tallahassee, ram Anthony Cooper off the road, quickly sedate him and then bring him to the island at Ben's request. Such an arrangement wouldn't be, well... very magic box-ish.

Assuming that the island manufactures things based upon the experiences of those who dwell upon it, this raises questions about everything we've seen so far. Could the oldest inhabitants of the island have been of Egyptian descent? The temple structures and hieroglyphics seem to point in that direction. If this were true, what were their beliefs? Did they believe in a god-monster made from tendrils of black smoke, who mercilessly passes judgement? Could enough people with a strong enough belief in something like that cause the island to actually *create* the smoke monster? Or was it here way before they even arrived, incorporated into their own system of beliefs after they encountered it?

The whole idea gives new meaning to Kate's words in *Outlaws*, where she tells Sawyer "I want carte blanche (blank check)." In effect the whole island becomes a blank check... a clean slate... a place much like the cave on Dagobah where Yoda is training a young, impetuous Luke Skywalker. What's in there? "Only what you bring with you."

Manifestation and Faith

Faith is one of the bigger aspects of LOST's story, and it plays a huge part in how things seem to work on the island. We've seen dozens of instances where truly believing in something has actually had a hand in making it happen. From Jack believing he could fix Sarah's broken spine to Hurley believing he could pop the clutch on a van that's been rotting in the jungle for over twenty years, having faith that something will actually occur seems to be the key to getting things done - both on and off the island.

As a doctor, we've seen Jack do some miraculous things. Back in episode one he brought Rose back to life with some simple CPR, but she'd just survived a plane crash so it was easy to swallow. Later on Jack stops Shannon's asthma attack seemingly through sheer force of will, and Hurley even accuses him of having Jedi-like powers. But the real kicker comes after Jack and Kate discover what appears to be a very dead Charlie hanging from a tree after his unfortunate encounter with Ethan in *All The Best Cowboys Have Daddy Issues*.

Watch that scene carefully. Jack spends several minutes pounding on Charlie's chest, shouting "come on!" and commanding him to "breathe!" When it becomes obvious that he's gone, Kate convinces Jack to stop. He does, and she tells him it's okay. For a moment it looks as if Jack's accepted the situation for what it is, but suddenly he gets it in his head that he can somehow still save his friend. Jack shoves Kate away and begins pounding on Charlie violently, over and over again, *demanding* that he wake up. And then suddenly, from out of nowhere, Charlie gasps for air and starts breathing again.

So the question becomes this: did Charlie really die here? Was Jack able to somehow resurrect him by simply *believing* he could be saved? If this was the time and place Charlie was supposed to kick off, it would definitely make a lot of sense later on in the story. Desmond's visions of Charlie's many deaths could simply be the island's way of course-correcting for the fact that Charlie was already supposed to be gone from the whole equation. By that point, you could argue that he wasn't supposed to be there at all.

After Jack brings him back, Charlie actually goes into a sort of trance where he doesn't say anything for quite some time. Later on during *Special*, he complains strangely: "Ever since Claire's gone it feels like bits of me are crumbling or something." And in *Whatever the Case May Be*, Rose tries to comfort him. When she points out that he came very close to dying for Claire, Charlie looks at her and says "Maybe I *should have* died." Taken by themselves, each of these scenes might not mean so much. But when strung together over the course of several episodes, you could easily make a case for Charlie actually dying at the hands of Ethan. For the rest of his time on the island, death surrounds Charlie. No matter what he does, he can't seem to escape it. In the end Charlie bravely embraces his fate, and when this happens it almost seems a relief for him.

Another important scene occurs during *Do No Harm*, where Boone releases Jack of his promise to save him. "Jack, let me go", Boone tells him. But then he looks up at Jack and says something strange and extremely interesting: "Look where we are."

Would Boone have lived if Jack didn't let him go? Would the amputation of his leg - which Jack was convinced would work - have kept Boone alive, or would Jack's faith have done that? Even more of a mystery: did Boone ask to be let go because of something he saw? We've seen characters most able to commune with the island while either sleeping, dreaming, or in a state of semi-awareness. As Boone slips in and out of consciousness, does he somehow "see" exactly where he is? Because if you watch that scene carefully, it looks as if Boone knew or was enlightened by something at the end. His final words to Jack were cryptic, and his last message to Shannon abruptly cut off... perhaps even by the island itself.

Jack's extraordinary healing powers seem to extend off-island as well. In *Man of Science, Man of Faith*, we're led to believe Jack's high rate of success is based upon his refusal to fail - a side effect of his very unforgiving upbringing. When faced with the no-win situation of Sarah's paralysis however,

Jack takes the very realist approach of knowing she'll never walk again. This is where Christian Shephard pulls him aside and schools Jack in the ways of hope. The lesson seems to stick, because almost in defiance of her condition Jack promises Sarah that he *will* fix her broken spine. Watch the scene in which this happens. He does it out of the clear blue sky, as if he were somewhere (or someone) else for a moment. Yet when he snaps back to reality, it's something Jack immediately regrets doing. When the operation is over, he heads out to both punish himself for making such a promise and to run off his aggression.

At the stadium, Jack meets Desmond. After a brief talk, Jack explains how he failed to fulfill the promise he made to his patient. Desmond oddly suggests that Jack *did* succeed in fixing Sarah. He talks about miracles, and for the second time in the episode, Jack is given a lesson in hope. He returns to the hospital, and Sarah begins wiggling her toes. By some miracle, Jack has managed to do exactly what he said he would.

It could be argued that Desmond's own faith helped heal Sarah here (especially if, like me, you don't think this is Desmond's first time meeting Jack). Even as he tries to explain his failure to Sarah, Jack is apologetic and still doubting his success. Still, he did *promise* to fix her. Jack went into the operation not only hoping to help Sarah's condition, but fully intending to get her to walk again. This type of faith seems to always win out, season after season, all throughout LOST. No matter what the odds, or how much of a longshot it might be, believing in the success of something is often all that is really needed to make it happen.

So did Jack's faith help him succeed? Did his belief that he *could* help his future wife nudge the die roll into that 1% margin of success? Other evidence points to that conclusion as well. Take Ben's approach to getting Jack to perform his own spinal surgery back in season three. When Jack asks him "You want me to save your life?", Ben tells him "No, I want you to *want* to save my life." On the island, where everything operates around the concept of faith, there is a huge difference between these two things. There were probably ten different ways Ben could've gotten Jack to operate on him, but he was adamant about getting Jack motivated about succeeding before anything else.

And let's go one step further. After the crash, Rose fully believes her husband is alive. She demonstrates unwavering faith to both Jack and Charlie that he wasn't killed in the plane crash. When asked "Do you think your husband is alive?", Rose calmly responds, "I know he is. There's a fine line between denial and faith. Believe me, it's better on my side."

Could you chalk up Bernard's very survival to Rose's firm belief that he lives? Did the island gently place him in that tree during *The Other 48 Days*, as a manifestation of Rose's total faith? It seems far fetched, but we *are* talking about LOST here. With Jack's shoeless father wandering zombie-like through the jungle, we've seen much stranger things.

And what about Dr. Leslie Arzt? No one was more sure that the dynamite found in the Black Rock would explode if handled. He moved it so slowly, so gingerly... he believed that at any moment, the whole thing would blow up. But did he believe it too much? Did Arzt manifest his own death by hyping up the danger level to such a degree that he unintentionally willed the nitroglycerine to go off? Because once he was gone, Jack and Locke had no trouble running full-tilt through the jungle carrying that same dynamite on their backs. Hurley handled it later on during *Everybody Hates Hugo*, and Rousseau carried off a whole box of it in *The Brig*. Once Arzt was done *believing* that the dynamite was radically unstable, it became a whole lot easier to deal with. Was the explosion a manifestation of Arzt's fear, or just coincidence?

Maybe on LOST, there are no coincidences. Maybe everything you see is placed into being by requirement, via the island's ability to create what's needed. Locke has an urgent need to open the hatch and suddenly there's a ship full of dynamite. Charlie's going through withdrawals, and there happens to be a planeload of heroin. Hurley's looking for something to turn his luck around when he stumbles across that Dharma van, and Sawyer's looking to replace his missing scotch when that van happens to be full of beer - beer that is somehow drinkable even after spending two decades in the sweltering heat. And when Sun needs a pregnancy test in *The Whole Truth*? One conveniently springs into existence. Kate even starts to question it: "Where did Sawyer find one of these anyway? I mean, who flies with a pregnancy test, right?" Right.

While suggestive manifestation doesn't explain everything on LOST, it's certainly something to be considered. It definitely seems to occur, but on what level does it go too far? At what point do you draw the line between calling things real or imaginary? Does Hurley's incessant hunger stock the pantry in the Swan hatch with tons of food? And when he destroys his stash, does the island tempt him with more by providing a phantom food drop? The island may be handing our characters the tools they need to accomplish certain tasks, but it can't seem to force them against free will. It gives them just enough to influence their decisions, but ultimately those decisions still seem to belong to them.

Assuming the island is pro-fate, and The Others are agents working to achieve its goals, it seems to want to maintain a certain historical path. Yet if sheer force of will can actually change or modify certain things, the island's innate abilities as a blank check would seem to undermine that whole agenda. The characters could, if they understood how things worked, change just about anything they wanted to. With true faith and belief, the rules could be bent - not just by the players of LOST's game, but seemingly by the very pieces on the game board as well. Looking at the final scenes of season five, there were a half-dozen people who really *believed* that the actions they were taking would be able to change the past. And with Juliet convinced she could set off a nuclear bomb by banging on it with a rock, maybe that's just what she did.

Perhaps we got our biggest clue to this in *316*, when Jack opened his hand to find only a scrap of John Locke's suicide note. The rest of the note was conveniently torn away, except for two very interesting words: "I wish." Considering the nature of what we've seen so far, this seems pretty important.

Does this theory reduce the island to little more than a wish-machine? Of course not. But looking ahead to season six, I think our main characters are going to have some very strong convictions. They've been through an awful lot, and they've learned much about the way things on the island seem to work. If they come to the realization that their faith and belief in things can shape future events - something that's probably not far off - this might be how they can take charge of their own destiny. As John Locke tells Walt in *Special*, "Picture it in your mind's eye. See it before you do it."

The Flashbacks Aren't Really Flashbacks

"Have we met?"
- Juliet to Ethan, *Not in Portland*

"Where do I know you from?"
- Desmond to Charlie, *Flashes Before Your Eyes*

"Small world, huh?"
- Sawyer to Jack, *Exodus Part 1*

"Is the reason you're so upset because he said he recognized you? Because that would be impossible."
- John Locke to Jack, *Orientation*

If the island is really creating manifestations of our characters' thoughts, hopes, and fears, the next natural step is to question the flashbacks themselves. By now we've seen multiple flashbacks, and in some cases even flash-forwards, for all of our main characters. It's not exactly clear if the flashbacks actively occur in the minds of these characters during each of their centric episodes, or whether we're just being shown glimpses of past history for the purposes of storytelling. Either way, we've seen some pretty fantastic stuff.

The staggering amount of coincidences within these flashbacks should be enough to make even the most casual viewer cry foul, yet the parallels keep on coming anyway. Episode after episode we've seen characters pop in and out of each other's flashbacks in ways that couldn't possibly be chalked up to sheer coincidence or simple chance. And aside from the characters themselves recurring, you've got places, objects, look-alikes, and even songs repeating themselves over and over again throughout the show - all of these occurring within flashbacks ranging from very recent events to childhood memories.

What's strange is that many people who watch LOST might question the on-island events, yet they treat the flashbacks as gospel. For some reason they seem to trust these pre-island memories as fact, as if the characters having island-influenced memories would be too dirty a trick for the writers to pull on them. Some have gone as far as to say they'd feel cheated or wronged by any tampering that occurs within the flashbacks and flash-forwards. These viewers want at least one unchangeable area of the show to hold onto - one solid thing they can trust - and maybe they can't be blamed for that. But if it turns out that everything in the flashbacks doesn't happen exactly as it occurred during the characters' lifetimes? Some type of hell is going to definitely break loose.

At this point, I think the idea that the flashbacks have been tampered with isn't even a question anymore. Watching Locke's Geiger counter migrate from his apartment in *Walkabout* to Desmond's shelf in the Swan hatch is suspicious enough, but seeing MacCutcheon's whisky - and *only* MacCutcheon's whisky - appear on the island, in the airport bar, and in multiple character flashbacks seems a little bit beyond belief. In the beginning these coincidences were fun and even funny, like Boone passing Sawyer in the Sydney police station, or the television showing Hurley's lottery win in the background during *In Translation*. Later on however, they got more and more over the top. You can't watch the same old brown Pontiac slam into Michael (*Special*), hit Locke (*Deus Ex Machina*), pull out in front of Kate (*Born to Run*), and then end Hurley's car chase (*The Beginning of The End*) without realizing that something is definitely up with the flashbacks. Something big.

After all, what are the chances that Ana Lucia and Sawyer just *happen* to meet Christian Shephard, who just *happens* to be Jack's dad, who just *happens* to be Claire's half-brother? And what are the odds that Ana Lucia almost hits Sawyer with her car door? That Desmond runs into Charlie in the streets of London? That Charlie saves Nadia from a mugger?

Conspiracy theory can only go so far here. There are people who steadfastly believe that when Juliet's ex husband got hit by that bus, Richard Alpert or one of his henchmen was behind the wheel. There are those who think someone really ran Cooper's car off the road just outside of Tallahassee. Some viewers conclude that Libby was intentionally planted at Santa Rosa mental hospital to keep an eye on Hurley, and then gave Desmond a boat so he could reach the island. And hey, maybe Brother Campbell even dated Eloise Hawking, since his desk displays a photo of the two of them together? At some point you have to admit that none of these things add up, even "coincidentally."

A good part of LOST's magic is that many of these things are inexplicable. They can't be reasonably accounted for, even by applying obscene amounts of logic. There was another television show that tried to go this route, and that was the *X-Files*. A great show with some great ideas, the *X-Files* started out with an eerie mystique that captured huge audiences and kept them spellbound with tales of the supernatural. By the end of the show however, it had abandoned the very principals that made it popular in the first place. Faith went out the window, as Mulder and Scully fully embraced science. A messy, messy conspiracy followed - one that stretched the limits of believability and involved everything from alien life-forms to underground government organizations hellbent on secrecy and cures for cancer. The show lost its audience by stomping all over its own magic. It tried to explain everything away in rational, logical terms instead of leaving something to the viewer's imagination.

In the words of the poster on Mulder's wall, "I want to believe." I'd like to think LOST won't go that route, and that the ending of the show will stay true to the way it began. That being said, the scenes and events that make up our characters' flashbacks have not only defied logic, they also raise some interesting questions about the validity of what we're being shown. Kate being a fan of Patsy Kline may be one thing, but hearing those songs on the radio just about every single time she flashes back is quite another. And while LOST's infamous "numbers" were almost a season one running joke, they became an integral part of the storyline when they kept showing up within everyone's flashbacks, appearing on everything from seat numbers to soccer jerseys, odometers and more.

But accepting our main characters' past memories as "pure" runs into a real snag when some of their flashbacks seem to contain impossible connections to the island. The cat Sayid remembers in his *Enter 77* flashback can't possibly be the same cat he spots outside the Flame Station, yet it sure as hell looks that way. If we're to believe the island didn't physically bring the cat there so much as Sayid created it, it becomes a manifestation of his guilt for what he did to his torture victim, Amira. It's a simple enough explanation which also jives with the fact that Mikhail names the cat Nadia - another very important figure in Sayid's life.

Yet along the same lines, let's examine an even more perplexing scenario that bridges the gap between flashback and on-island reality. Jack meeting Desmond while running his Tour de Stade can be chalked up as two strangers who bump into each other while exercising. Yet when they run into each other again on the island, the coincidence is just too overwhelming. They can't logically *both* be there, which leaves the possibility that one (or both) of them are figments of the other's imagination. Did the island create Desmond from Jack's own thoughts? Or was it vice versa? Or could it be that they're both living, breathing souls that just happened to arrive on the same island together, thousands of miles from where they managed to cross paths the first time?

Tossing that idea aside, the only other reasonable explanation is that higher powers brought them together each time - both on and off the island. This might fit in well with LOST's theme of predetermination and inescapable destiny, but even that falls short of explaining other odd occurrences within the flashbacks. For example, take the artwork we see throughout the show. Why do the paintings done by Claire's boyfriend Thomas in *Raised by Another* look so similar to the mural in the Swan hatch? In fact, one of Thomas's exact paintings shows up behind Desmond as he sits in Charles Widmore's office two seasons later. This is a flashback-to-flashback parallel, one that's perpetuated even further on the walls of Widmore's bedroom in season four. If we accept the flashbacks as unmanipulated fact, we have to at least agree that the likelihood of such a similarity taking place is borderline astronomical.

Episode after episode, season after season, we keep getting slapped in the face with impossible coincidences - both within the flashbacks and outside of them. We're given duplicate scenes, places, names, people, and items. Similarities are rife on LOST, but even more interesting are the similar appearances we've seen between our main characters and the less significant one-shot throwaway roles throughout the show. How can Ben look so much like Claire's ex-boyfriend Thomas, Charlie's brother Liam look so much like Nadia's mugger, and Claire look so much like the blonde woman who finds Aaron in the grocery store? Going one step beyond, Jack looks *nearly identical* to Mathias (one of the Portuguese members of the tracking station in *Live Together, Die Alone*), and Sawyer seems to be sitting across from his doppleganger during the security meeting in *He's Our You*. Even the title of that last episode seems to smugly hint at some manner of duplicity. It's as if there's a lookalike or replacement for everyone, from the younger version of Mr. Eko looking like the photo of Mrs. Gardner's grandson in *Confirmed Dead*, to Mr. Friendly (a.k.a. Tom) looking eerily similar to Mike, the leader of Locke's commune in *Further Instructions*.

Just as the same brown Pontiac keeps appearing within (and altering the course of) several character flashbacks, it's no coincidence that a car wreck prevents Jack from jumping off the Sixth Street Bridge in *Through the Looking Glass*. Similarly, it's no coincidence that the bandaged-up woman involved in the wreck looks almost identical to Sarah, Jack's ex-wife. As always, Jack's need to save someone overrides his own personal agenda here, diverting him from suicide and completing an inner loop of his own. But the important thing to realize is that no matter where we are in the story - flashbacks, flash-forwards, or even the on-island present - some type of outside forces seem to have a definite hand in shaping and molding the scenery. And it always seems to happen in some sort of circular manner.

The Islands Own Version of Events

So are the past events of our character's lives being manipulated by outside forces, or are the flashbacks themselves being tampered with? Is it possible that the pre-island memories we've been seeing for so long aren't 100% genuine representations of how things really went down? On an even more sinister level, could the flashbacks be nothing but total bullshit? Trumped-up roles created specifically by the island to account for each of our character's past lives?

It's an interesting theory, and one with a good amount of supporting evidence. If the island is even partially giving birth to what we see in the flashbacks, it would account for a ton of interesting parallels and impossible coincidences. It would explain why we see repeating roles, storylines, items, and dialogue. It would justify how Sayid knew both Sam Austen and Kelvin Inman even before he got to the island. It would rationalize how Randy Nations could be both Hurley's boss at the Mr. Cluck's Chicken Shack, and Locke's supervisor at the box company. It would explain how the horse statue on Ben's bookcase in *The Man From Tallahassee* ends up behind Desmond in the Oxford library during *Jughead*.

Imagine for a moment that the island works almost like a database, and that within that database is a finite amount of information from which it can draw upon. Let's say this information is limited to the memories, events, and knowledge it receives from those who arrived upon its shores. The island therefore has names it can use, faces it knows, places it can recreate... but its abilities are limited only to those things. As it tampers with and draws up memories for the character flashbacks, it keeps repeating certain objects and events over and over again. Scenarios, motifs, phraseology - all of them being used again and again as the island tries to provide every character with his or her own unique experience.

So now take Jenna the gate attendant who phones someone named "Hunter" to let Hurley on Flight 815. When she shows up four seasons and a whole continent later as a receptionist named Moira in Desmond's flashback (*Jughead*), it's not so surprising anymore. She could be an agent of the island, guiding the main characters along the path of destiny... or she could be nothing more than an "extra" provided by the island to fill certain roles within these flashbacks. Her duty changes, her name changes, but her appearance remains the same.

Similarly, what if the island only knew certain brand names, like Apollo candy bars and MacCutcheon's whiskey? As it modified or altered the character flashbacks, it would have to use these names anywhere and everywhere they were applicable. It would make sense that they would repeat over and over again, because the island is limited to using only what it knows. But could it create other names as well? Would it take existing words and scramble them to form anagrams like Mittelos (lost time) Bioscience? Herarat (Earhart) Aviation? Hoffs/Drawlar (flash-forward) funeral parlor? Canton Rainier (reincarnation) carpet cleaning?

The above examples are probably little more than cute hints given to us by the writers of LOST. Still, the naming convention that the island uses definitely seems to be limited - especially when it comes to character names. Common names like Tom and Michael aren't very shocking - they're bound to be repeated given the sheer number of characters we've seen so far. Still, that doesn't explain the recycling of uncommon names such as Nadler, Oldham, Carlyle, Lapidus, and many others. Each of those examples have appeared more than once throughout the show. Whether they're used to describe the names of people, places, towns or corporations doesn't really matter... the important thing is that the island seems stuck with these words and has to use them where it can.

And what does the island do when it doesn't have a name for something? It creates convenient parallels, like Sun's pregnancy test being manufactured by "Widmore Labs." Like the bullets Kate finds in the basement of the Flame station bearing the brand name "Marshal." You could even go a step further with this theory, suggesting that maybe Dharma is the generic, no-frills brand name it uses to fill in for all the other items it doesn't know about. Hurley's ranch dressing, the cereal... we've even seen Dharma theatrical glue for Mr. Friendly's fake beard. Sawyer's trying to find out who drank his alcohol when he stumbles across a van loaded with Dharma beer.

It's funny how these sort of things always seem to work out, too. In season two, we find a glass eye, and in season three, a man who's missing one. Virtually anything that needs an explanation is conveniently manufactured. In *Enter 77* we see generic Dharma boxes containing generic Dharma binders right next to a whole row of Dharma jumpsuits. One of the binders contains information that seems to rationalize the food drop - one of the bigger mysteries at that point. Yet as Mikhail pours lemonade and serves up Dharma crackers, our survivors are smart enough to balk. As Kate even says that episode, "It just doesn't make sense."

By now we've seen enough of Dharma to know that all of this is standard operating procedure. Still, doesn't it seem a little too convenient that decades later the Swan's whole pantry is filled with such products, from the peanut butter right down to the mac and cheese? Isn't it strange how Geronimo Jackson's records and posters keep showing up in various places throughout various timelines? How the same old songs keep playing again and again? Desmond spins *Make Your Own Kind of Music* by Mama Cass in the Swan hatch, then suspiciously encounters it again in the pub... Juliet plays *Downtown* by Petula Clark at the barracks, but we hear it again on the radio during her flashback in *One of Us*. This is the island's own limited record collection, and apparently we're stuck with it.

Mistakes and Corrections

The island isn't perfect, either. Going back to Brother Campbell for a moment, look a little more closely at the photo on his desk. Not only do he and Ms. Hawking both appear in front of the monastery, but it looks like they were Photoshopped into the picture by a six-year old kid using the cropping tool for the very first time. Neither one of them really belongs - it's as if the island jammed them in there as an afterthought, a hastily added detail it didn't take the time to fully work out. And this isn't the only photo the island screws up, either. Noticed by just about everyone, the array of photos on Mrs. Gardner's wall during *Confirmed Dead* all leap out and switch frames between the time Miles goes upstairs to speak to her dead grandson and the time he comes back down. This goes way beyond simple set error: multiple photos have multiple different frames. The writers and producers of LOST may be pulling the wool over our eyes for the past five years, but every once in a while they intentionally show us something. Whether or not we choose to look is entirely up to us.

Another big piece of evidence for the falsification of the flashbacks occurs during Desmond's apparent journey through time in *Flashes Before Your Eyes*. This was the episode that knocked us on our ass in terms of what we knew, and what we thought we knew. In it, Desmond appears to be thrown back into his own past, waking up to eerily notice that the microwave in his flat sounds suspiciously like the countdown clock for the Swan hatch. This is impossible of course... yet there it is - an exact audio replica of what he would experience in his button-pushing future. As he walks dream-like through his own past, Desmond maintains bits and pieces of his future-past consciousness. And just as he thinks maybe he's been given a second chance at doing things right in life, along comes Ms. Hawking - agent of the island - to convince him otherwise.

But was Desmond actually plucked from the present and embedded in the past? Did he really travel through time when the Swan hatch imploded? Or is Desmond being *shown* everything that he sees and experiences, instead? Could it be possible that Desmond's turning of the failsafe key actually launched him into a *broken* flashback - one where he could still interact with those around him - while maintaining memories of his previous life?

Such a theory would explain an even more important aspect of Desmond flashing through time: the fact that he apparently brought future knowledge back with him. As he gets cast back into the "real" timeline again, Desmond undergoes an island-induced rebirth process and is imbued with knowledge of events that haven't even happened yet. His future vision is obscured however, coming only in bits and pieces. This type of thought-scrambling exactly mirrors the way Desmond could only remember bits and pieces of his time on the island. After his initial flash, Desmond only vaguely remembered Charlie when he met him on the streets of London, and got the dates mixed up on the Graybridge soccer game. If those were actual memories, that would make his precognitive visions memories as well - but ones from the future instead of the past.

So has Desmond already lived out the ending of LOST and somehow forgotten it? Or is the entire timeline already predetermined, with Desmond accidentally being shown glimpses of it during his rewind and subsequent fast-forward through the time arc? Whatever the case, we're led to believe that Desmond v.2.0 is uniquely special. He's demonstrated the ability to change or modify the future through his attempts to save Charlie, and we've seen the island respond by frantically scrambling to course-correct.

If you buy into the theory that the flashbacks aren't real, then maybe the future isn't real either. And instead of the well-laid plans the island has in store for everyone, we're going to see that Desmond's actions have thrown a wrench in the works. By keeping Charlie alive long enough to flip the jamming switch in the Looking Glass, he indirectly brought the freighter to the island in season four. This set into motion the series of events that lead to the rescue of the O6, Locke turning the frozen donkey wheel, and perhaps even the spawning of a whole new timeline in season six... one in which Flight 815 doesn't crash at all. That's something we'll just have to see.

In the end, I think there's a pretty good chance we'll get an answer for what exactly the flashbacks might be. The list of connections between the characters used to resemble a spider web, but by now it's nothing more than a chaotic, tangled mess. They've crossed paths simply too many times. We've seen way too many duplicates; too many look-alikes and repeats to believe that even "fate" is responsible for so many parallels. Asking us to accept the character flashbacks as established fact is a little too much at this point, so if you're looking for the man behind the curtain you're definitely not alone.

Everyone's Dead...
They're all in Purgatory

"Three days ago, we all died."
- Jack, *Tabula Rasa*

"There are no survivors. This is our life now. Get used to it."
- Ana Lucia, *The Other 48 Days*

"This place is death!"
- Charlotte, *This Place is Death*

"Don't let the air conditioning fool you, son. You are here, too. You are suffering."
- Christian Shephard, *Outlaws*

It's one of the oldest and most popular theories of season one, and it was the quickest theory to be shot down by the writers and producers of LOST. But right from the very beginning, even before things went totally crazy... it certainly seemed as if everyone on the island were already dead.

The idea that everyone died in the crash of Flight 815 is as simple as it is chilling. With everyone dead and the island acting as each person's own individual Purgatory, the story could take on a life of its own. It would give the scriptwriters free reign over whatever happened next, the license to induce strange visions, create monsters, animate the dead, and do pretty much whatever they hell they wanted to. Anything and everything could happen, and it could all be wrapped up with a logical explanation when, at the series finale, it was revealed exactly where our characters were the whole time.

The problem with this theory is that it's a little too simple. It's a little too self-serving, too. While it would make (and has made) a great thirty-minute episode of *The Twilight Zone*, it seems a little too short and obvious for LOST. At a quick glance, it would explain just about everything. It would account for why each of the characters seems to be on a journey of self-discovery, reflecting back upon their pre-island lifetimes via the flashbacks. As each individual person realizes their mistakes or reconciles the obstacles they've faced during life, they're rewarded with "death" by being allowed to pass on into another life. Boone, Shannon, Charlie, Ana Lucia... all of these characters realized their faults and atoned for them in some way, and shortly afterward they died on the island.

Such a theory would also explain why the children Zach and Emma - and later on Walt and Aaron - were taken. Young and innocent, they'd be exempt from serving time in purgatory because they hadn't been exposed to the corruption of everyday adult life. In the words of Goodwin, "They're better off now." This also gels with why certain "good" people disappeared rather quickly, whether they were dragged off into the jungle as in *The Other 48 Days* or suddenly drowned like Joanna in *White Rabbit*.

In fact, Joanna becomes even more interesting when you examine some seemingly throwaway dialogue from Kate. In talking to Jack about her, Kate tells him "She wasn't supposed to be on the plane. She was scuba diving off the barrier reef and got an ear infection so the doctor grounded her for two days. She bumped her flight. That's how she ended up with us." Assuming this was true, Joanna was dragged out to sea in much the same way many of the tail section survivors were dragged into the jungle. If she wasn't supposed to be part of the plane crash, perhaps Joanna wasn't supposed to be part of LOST's story at all.

Since new souls wouldn't be created in Purgatory, this would further explain why babies cannot be born on the island. It could account for the island's uncanny healing properties, and for the fact that cancer and other diseases don't seem to exist. Even pre-existing conditions like Rose's terminal cancer or John Locke's paralysis seem to disappear, allowing the characters to prove or disprove themselves unfettered by the baggage or injuries brought with them from previous lifetimes.

JJ Abrams first debunked the Purgatory theory in March 2005, when fans everywhere thought they had LOST figured out. Back then the show was brimming with references to the characters being dead, especially in season one, with most of these being made by the main characters themselves. Jack and Locke both talk about everyone dying and being reborn on the island with a clean slate. In talking to Kate during *The Moth*, Sayid questions how they could've possibly lived through the crash, after the fuselage "cartwheeled through the jungle", leaving everyone "with only a few scrapes." When Kate suggested their survival was dumb luck, Sayid was quick to stop her: "No one's that lucky. We shouldn't have survived."

Even more interesting are the strange and out of place references to death and the afterlife. Some of these are buried within dialogue that goes by rather quickly, but upon deeper analysis just seems plain weird. In *Collision*, Ana Lucia releases Sayid from captivity and tells him "What good would it do to kill you when we're both already dead?" Her choice of words doesn't exactly fit here, and seems more like a subtle nod to the idea that none of the characters ever survived the plane crash. Ditto for Michael's words to Jack in *Solitary*: "I was an artist in a previous life." Not exactly damning proof that Michael considers his past life over, but his words are strange against the context. Desmond uses the phrase "another life" very frequently, as does Nadia when she writes Sayid's note on the back of her photo.

Other subtle clues exist also. In *Solitary*, Sawyer accuses Jack of patching him up just so he can "get into heaven." When Anthony Cooper eludes to Sawyer that they're all in hell, Sawyer responds with "Oh okay, so we're dead?" All throughout the show, multiple references are made to the idea that the characters must choose their own path, make their own decisions, and do things all on their own. It's almost as if influencing them would be defeating the purpose of each person proving themselves by finding his or her own way. In *Hearts and Minds*, Locke is driven by the island to test Boone. He does this by binding him, and then giving Boone all the tools necessary to free himself not only physically, but also mentally from the self-imposed bonds of his sister Shannon. "You need to let go of a few things", Locke tells him. "You'll be able to cut yourself free when you have the proper motivation."

Shortly after Boone frees himself, he dies, just as Shannon dies shortly after she allows herself to love someone unconditionally. Ana Lucia is allowed to pass on after reconciling her anger over the man who killed her unborn child. Charlie dies after finally accepting responsibility for someone other than himself. As each of these people "find" themselves they are no longer LOST, and therefore no longer need to serve out time on the island... whether it be Purgatory, Limbo, hell, or some other form of punishment.

And punishment it is, too. Even the characters get a direct sense that they've screwed up their previous lives, and may be living out some form of torment for their misdeeds. "I'm in this place because I'm being punished", Jin tells Sun before getting on the raft in *Exodus*. "I made you suffer. You don't deserve any of this." The raft is small penance for what Jin thinks he's done, but he'd rather face it than endure the shame of having wronged his wife. In *Special*, Walt even mentions that building the raft "feels like punishment."

This sort of redemption process is a part of LOST, whether the island turns out to be Purgatory or not. Even as both Damon Lindelof and Carlton Cuse went on further denounce the theory that the characters were in some sort of afterlife, they've also stated that the show is indeed about people resolving the issues of their pre-island lives. They do this by battling their inner demons, seemingly with the help and guidance of the island, the smoke monster, and whatever other forces are at work.

As debunked it can possibly be, even the writers won't let the Purgatory theory die off completely. Deep into season three, Naomi teases us with the real-world knowledge that Flight 815 really did crash, and that there were no survivors. We're even shown footage of the wreckage, and then promptly led to believe that it's false. But before you take the plane in the Sunda Trench and chalk it up as part of an elaborate conspiracy, ask yourself this: how is it that after sinking 5 miles deep, the aircraft just *happened* to break into the same three pieces - cockpit, fuselage, and tail section - as the "real" Flight 815 that crashed on the island? If Charles Widmore really did go through the trouble of staging the wreckage, how could he have gotten something like that correct, without any knowledge of the crash itself?

If the writers and producers of LOST are flat out lying, I

can't say I blame them. Admitting that viewers have finally solved the show certainly isn't an option, no matter what season we're in. But even if the creators of LOST aren't lying, they seem to love to tease us with the idea that the characters are trapped in a post-life Limbo. In *Something Nice Back Home*, Hurley flat out tells Jack: "We're dead. All of us. All the Oceanic Six, we're all dead. We never got off that island." It doesn't get much more direct than that.

So is everyone on the island really dead? Were the Oceanic Six never supposed to leave the island because they're already deceased, and can't truly exist in the real world? Or will course correction change everyone's fate, with Juliet's detonation of Jughead causing a big enough ripple in the stream of time to change the way the entire show plays out? Season six will show us these things, and we might be surprised by what we see. We may just find out that we agree with Locke, who tells us "survival is relative" way back in season one. Death is certainly a relative term, especially when it comes to the island. And what we thought might be Purgatory may turn out to be something completely different.

The Future of The Purgatory Theory

Decried by every major creator of the show year in and year out, the future of the purgatory theory looks pretty grim. That's not to say we might not see some variation of this theory, where the characters are explained to be lost in some otherworldly Limbo without really being dead at all. With heavy doses of reincarnation and karma spattered throughout LOST, even reinserting the spiritually enlightened characters back into the real world would be a form of rebirth, fulfilling the whole idea of "see you in another life."

Another way for the writers to duck out of their constant assertions that the characters are alive and well would be the explanation of alternate timelines: one in which Flight 815 reached the island, the other in which it never crashed at all. If everything the characters were trying to accomplish comes to fruition in season six, we might end up seeing that no one ever really died - not even the people we've seen killed with our own eyes.

Still, the island has to be *something*. I can't imagine the show ending without explaining at least a little bit about the origins of the island, where it came from, and why it doesn't seem to be part of the natural world. I don't think we need every gory detail, but when that last LOST logo slams across our screens, I think we're owed at least some kind of rough definition as to where we've spent the last six years. But will it be Purgatory? Probably not.

LOST is a Big Game Being Played by Two Sides

"You like to play games John?"
- Jack, *Exodus Part 2*

"Two players. Two sides. One is light, one is dark."
- John Locke, *Pilot Part 2*

"This isn't a game, man."
- Hurley, *Hearts & Minds*

"Ready to play? Ready to play?"
- The Flame Station Computer, *Enter 77*

Dark vs. light. Black vs. white. Science vs. faith. Free will vs. fate. The never-ending duality of LOST runs rampant in every season, in just about every episode. It didn't take us long to realize a game was being played, and that the Flight 815 survivors were a part of that game. Since Locke and Walt began playing backgammon in the Pilot episode, we've seen all kinds of game references within the show.

Literally speaking, these games are everywhere. Locke's backgammon game is put to good use on the island, at least until Hurley gets everyone playing golf. Chess, horseshoes, ping pong, poker... all of these games are also played on the island, presumably to pass the time. And while it seems natural that the survivors would need activities like this to maintain their sanity, the game theme continues off island as well. In flashbacks we see Hurley playing Connect Four with Leonard at Santa Rosa, and John Locke playing war games with coworkers on his lunch break. The theme is even extended all the way up to the arctic listening station, with the two Portuguese staff members Henrik and Mathias playing chess at the exact moment the Swan hatch implosion turns the sky purple.

Most interesting of all however, is Locke's detailed explanation of the game Mouse Trap in *Deus Ex Machina*. Instead of playing it, he's actually demonstrating it to a child. This is where the game theme goes from literal to figurative, because the writers are making a definitive point here. As Locke talks about the piece-by-piece set up of the game board, parallels could be drawn to the entire storyline of LOST itself. One by one the island (or game board) has carefully placed the pieces (or characters) into position, waiting for that split second when the trap is finally sprung. In this respect, Mouse Trap becomes a very good analogy for the whole show, with the penultimate moment occurring when the mouse takes the cheese.

And isn't Mouse Trap really nothing but a long con itself? A long, involved process where everything must fall *exactly* into proper place in order for the end result to occur? As Jacob's dark-shirted nemesis tells him right before he drives Ben to kill him, "You have no idea what I've gone through to be here."

If LOST is nothing but a game being played by two or more sides, we need to examine who the players are. That seems simple enough, until you've watched five seasons of the show. As each season ends in an explosive finale, the smoke clears and we're left with the hint of a much bigger picture. The Flight 815 survivors vs. The Others battle of seasons one and two gives way to Benjamin Linus vs. Charles Widmore. This eventually gives way to Jacob vs. his nemesis. Yet even as Jacob dies, his last words "They're coming" seem to yield control to an even higher authority. So where does the chain of command finally come to an end? Are Jacob and his friend in the dark shirt controlling the many processes of the island, or is the island itself in control? And is there someone even above all of those things, when it comes to running the game?

Taken from a logical standpoint, *somebody* had to make the rules. Someone originally had to write up the Book of Laws, and it looks like everyone on the island now has to play by them. Even Jacob's nemesis can't outright kill him without finding a very complicated, long-winded loophole. That in itself says something important. It shows that even those two characters, higher up than anyone else we've seen so far, can't just run around doing whatever they want, whenever they want to.

Digging deeper into their conversation at the beginning of *The Incident*, it doesn't seem like either of them even want to play. Not anymore, at any rate. Jacob looks tired, but appears determined to find a way to win. To do this he needs to prove that humankind can do more than just kill, destroy, and corrupt. As he keeps bringing new playing pieces to the game board of the island, his opponent shows nothing but bitter contempt at the notion that Jacob's even attempting to continue. The dark-shirted man has totally had it. Each successive loop has always ended in a stalemate, and he doesn't want to play anymore. For him, the only way out is to kill Jacob and stop the game from continuing on, and so he gets to work on it. We're given the distinct impression that the game has gone on way too long, which may be why there's a good chance we're finally going to see the end of it.

So was Jacob the mouse, finally captured at the end of the game by his arch-rival? Probably not. It might be more likely that Jacob's nemesis unknowingly sprung the trap, and will soon realize that he's the one trapped in the cage. As long of a con he had to pull in order to get everything to fall into place, I have a feeling that he's the one who took the cheese. Because if you remember, in the game of Mouse Trap, *both* players set up the pieces of the game board. *Both* players have a hand in laying them down and making sure that everything fits. The ultimate winner of the game is the one who out-cons the other.

Yet beyond the simple one-on-one game of life and death that Jacob and his enemy seem to be playing, LOST also alludes to much bigger and more sinister end results. According to Ms. Hawking, ultimate champion of the "whatever happens, happens" campaign, Desmond must not change a single decision he makes or else "every single one of us will die." A bit overly dramatic, or does she know something that we don't? Her doomsaying ways are perpetuated again in *The Lie*, where she delivers the warning "God help us all" - a grim reminder to Ben of what would happen should he fail to get the Oceanic Six back to the island.

Apparently everyone's in for some real end-of-the-world type shit if things don't go down exactly the way they're supposed to. In the middle of season five, Charles Widmore's own words to John Locke seem to echo the concerns of Ms. Hawking, his ex-lover. When Locke asks why Widmore would go out of his way to help him get back to the island, he replies: "Because there's a war coming, John. And if you're not back on the island when that happens, the wrong side is going to win." Of course we're never given information as to who the two sides are and what the stakes might be, but that's LOST. In any case, the end result seems to be something that needs to be avoided at all costs.

Getting back to the game theme, there are several interesting elements to consider when it comes to opposing sides. We've seen characters switch roles numerous times throughout the story, going from one side to the other without rhyme or reason. We've seen characters or game pieces captured, frozen, and removed from play... but just as quickly we've seen them returned to play as well. The constant reappearance of Mikhail sticks out like a sore thumb; there was a time it seemed as if the guy simply couldn't be killed. Even beyond life we've seen the dead return to walk, speak, and interact with our living characters... and the fact that this mostly happens while they're sleeping, dreaming, unconscious, or drugged should not be lost on anyone watching the show.

Light and Dark... White and Black... Good and Evil

No matter what the story, the age-old battle between opposing forces always seems to be crystallized within this same recurring theme. From the moment Adam & Eve's black and white stones were held in Jack's palm, we knew that dark and light sides would be represented within the overall story. But look a little closer, and you can go back even earlier than that. Just minutes into the Pilot episode, we get the show's very first reference to dark and light. As Kate's about to stitch Jack's wound closed with the sewing kit, Jack can have any color thread he wants. But which one does he choose? "Standard black."

This seemingly unimportant moment also marks one of the

first concrete choices a character makes, all on his own. As the Flight 815 survivors work to eke out a life for themselves on the beach, The Others are scrambling to draw up lists and choose up sides. Some of the crash survivors would be marked as good, others would be labeled as bad. This seemed pretty important back in seasons one and two, with Goodwin actually "making a case" for Ana Lucia (according to Ben), and The Others targeting Mr. Eko as desirable... at least until he killed two would-be abductors with a rock. After that, Eko fell into a whole different category as far as The Others were concerned, which seemed to align their interests not just in terms of black and white, but also of saints and sinners.

But for the moment, let's assume the most logical thing: white represents good, and black represents evil. With The Others claiming to be the "good guys" does that make them part of the white team? At Colleen's funeral they're all wearing white robes, and at the end of season three they're marking tents with white rocks. By seasons four and five, the Flight 815 survivors and even some of the freighter crew are working right alongside The Others. Adding everything up, you could draw a rough conclusion that the team of people aligned with the island's interests (either willingly or unwillingly) seem to be associated mostly with the color white.

Taking that into consideration, it makes Jack's choice much more significant. Right from the very first episode, before the spinning engines of Flight 815 had even grown cold, he chose the color black. Is this what Isabel meant when, in *Stranger in a Strange Land*, she commented on Jack's tattoo? "He walks amongst us, but he is not one of us." Is that because on some unknown level, Jack's really a member of the opposing side?

We could go crazy knocking ourselves out with all the black and white references throughout LOST. While not everything is always significant, some clues stand out as just too big too ignore. The black and white stones Jack finds at the cave complex are seen replacing Locke's eyes during Claire's dream in *Raised by Another*. Interpreting this, it could mean that John Locke is a man divided: torn between both sides, perhaps even haunted (or occupied?) by forces both light and dark. Ditto for Sawyer's glasses, which Sayid creates by melting white and black plastic frames together. This is symbolic of Sawyer being on the fence; a bad man about to turn good. Of all LOST's characters you could argue that Sawyer has undergone the most radical of all transformations, a five-season metamorphosis from career criminal into upstanding citizen and head of Dharma security.

One of the more dramatic settings of black vs. white occurs at the end of *The Shape of Things to Come*, as Benjamin Linus confronts Charles Widmore in his own penthouse bedroom. Shadows are expertly manipulated to fall across Ben's face, bisecting it neatly down the nose line into two halves: one side falling into darkness, one exposed to the light. As Charles sits up in bed the same thing happens to him, only the opposite sides of his face are light and dark. Ben's right side is cloaked in darkness, but for Charles it's his left. This continues

LOST's "mirror" theme, representing the constant duality of the two sides and players in addition to continuing the black and white imagery.

This sort of visual ying and yang is constantly given nods in the black and white colors of the Swan's countdown clock, the design of the Dharma logos, in Charlie's checkered shoes, even in pairs of characters such as Rose and Bernard - two people who many fans already speculate will turn out to be the Adam & Eve skeletons we find in the caves during season one. From dominoes to dice, from one side of the chessboard to the other, the black vs. white theme has become symbolic of two opposing sides struggling against one another, as if one big game were being played.

And then finally, in the season five finale, we're given Jacob in a white shirt, and his nemesis in a black one. With all the twists and turns we've seen for the last five years, we can't expect to have been handed something so brutally obvious. It's little wonder that fans instantly began arguing over who's really good and who's really evil - it's not like we can trust the writers to make something this easy to figure out. But then again, maybe that's the genius of it all. After having thrown us curve ball after curve ball, maybe the writers thought a change-up was necessary to keep things interesting.

Mirrors and Reflections

Other symbols of contrast are peppered throughout the

show, particularly through the use of mirrors. We see an extraordinary number of mirrors in LOST, and some shots are even opened by shooting a character's image through a nearby mirror or reflection. There's the mirror used to reflect Jack's appendectomy, the one Ben uses to signal his people, the adjustable mirrors of the Swan hatch's security system, and at least a half-dozen scenes where a character (usually Jack without a shirt on) is reflected in a bathroom mirror, to name only a few. The reversed effects produced by mirror imagery do a great job of illustrating the flip-flopped, often backwards themes we see all through the show.

But in some cases, mirrors also seem to reflect back unwanted visions of a character that cause them great anger or sorrow. This is probably because the mirrored images represent something a little deeper for each character: the truth. Jin cries into a mirror during *In Translation*, when he sees himself covered in the blood of the man he's just beaten. Although he angrily tells Sun he's only doing what needs to be done to provide for his family, the mirror is unconvinced. It reflects back the truth of the matter: that Jin is no longer the good, innocent man he once was.

Kate looks into a full-length mirror in *I Do*. Upon seeing her reflection in a bridal gown, the truth hits home: she's still a fugitive wanted for murder. The inescapability of her situation strikes Kate hard at that very moment, and she makes the decision to leave her fiancé Kevin.

The same revelation happens in *The Economist*, where

Sayid is playing out a similar lie in his relationship with Elsa. As that situation blows up violently, Sayid smashes the mirror from which Elsa is watching him before shooting her dead. In both cases the mirror is representative of a life each character inwardly knows they can never have: their own lies are reflected back at them, showing them what they look like from the outside in. This causes them to realize the errors of pretending, and seems to drive them back along a predetermined (predestined?) path. Sayid's smashing of the mirror was indicative of him finally accepting the truth, and refusing to continue buying into the lie.

The mirror parallels are continued in *A Tale of Two Cities*. Juliet is playing the happy hostess and getting ready for her book club meeting. Once she looks into her mirror however, she begins to cry. Her reflection reminds her of who she really is: a prisoner being held against her will. Since arriving on the island everything in her life has been a lie, from her affair with Goodwin to Ben's never-ending deception that keeps her from leaving. No amount of pretending can cover up the real situation, reflected back upon her with brutal honesty by the mirror. And as if to pull her away from such truth and draw her back to the land of illusion, the island then has the balls to burn her muffins.

Facing the truth is a recurring theme on LOST, and the mirrors seem geared toward revealing a character's daydream or fallacy. In *The Beginning of the End*, Hurley drives his Camaro into a whole freestanding array of mirrors set up in the middle of nowhere, almost as if trying to show him the real deal... and if you believe another theory later on in this book about the off-island world of the Oceanic Six, those mirrors were placed there as an attempt to reflect one of the biggest lies of all. The same thing applies to the mirrored shot we get of Kate running desperately through the grocery store, trying to find Aaron in *Whatever Happened, Happened*. What we're seeing is the truth - the mirror is showing us things as they really are. Up until that point we were seeing the sugar-coated fantasy world of post-island Kate, one in which she gets let off the hook for murder and tries to play the role of super mom, potential wife, and happy homemaker.

Opposing Episode Titles

The titles of the episodes themselves often reflect polar opposites. After being given *The Constant* we eventually get *The Variable*. For *One of Them*, we have *One of Us*. Opposite *The Whole Truth* we're given an episode called *The Lie*.

We've even seen opposites within the same title: *Fire + Water*, *Hearts and Minds*, *Live Together Die Alone*, and *The Beginning of the End*. Throughout the show we've always been given the impression that there are two distinct sides being played upon one another, as if in a game. The writers have cleverly perpetuated this concept in choosing the names of each episode.

Two Different Smoke Monsters - Black and White

LOST's dichotomies may even extend all the way to the smoke monster itself, and once again in terms of black and white. It's almost as if we've seen two different versions of the creature: one that rips trees out by the roots, and one that takes the form of tendrils of black smoke. It's possible that both of these are actually the same monster, but it's just as possible that we're lumping together two separate entities with two separate goals. In rewatching the older episodes and knowing what we know now? There's more and more evidence that there may be two monsters.

The first clue comes with the descriptions given by both John Locke and Mr. Eko. Locke claims to have looked into the heart of the island, telling Jack "what I saw was beautiful." When he later tells Eko that he saw a "very beautiful bright light", Eko's disagrees completely with his account of the monster. He tells Locke simply, "That is not what I saw."

If there are two smoke monsters, one dark and one light, it would symbolically seem to fit right in. We already know that the black smoke monster appeared to Eko in the form of his brother Yemi, right before judging and then subsequently killing him. This would be the dark form seen also by Charlie, the monster that attacked Keamy's mercenaries in season four, and the one called "Cerberus" by the Dharma Initiative that chased Juliet and Kate through the sonic fence in *Left Behind*. Its ability to scan thoughts and represent itself as the dead also seems to indicate it has some kind of agenda all its own.

But what if there were an opposite creature, like the one John Locke saw and described? Was it another form of the smoke monster that morphed itself into Christian Shephard, leading Jack to both shelter and water in *White Rabbit*? Even the very title of that episode can be used to solidify the theory of a white smoke monster. Maybe this is the same creature that manifested itself as Kate's horse or Sawyer's boar, representations of freedom and guilt downloaded straight out of their past memories to help the characters along on their way to enlightenment. This would be the good monster - the one working to aid the Flight 815 survivors in passing the harsh judgment of its dark counterpart, much the way Locke helped Ben pass Cerberus' ultimate judgment in *Dead is Dead*.

Drawing connections to Jacob and his nemesis, think back to their opening scene on the beach. The dark-shirted man emerges from the jungle and Jacob offers him some fish. "No thanks", he tells him, "I just ate." This is an eerie and ominous statement... one that should remind us sharply of pilot Seth Norris getting torn through the cockpit window of Flight 815, or of Nadine's body falling to the ground as Rousseau's science expedition first ran from the monster. If Jacob and his opponent turn out to be some sort of ageless demigods pitted against one another, maybe they control or are actually representations of the smoke monster(s) themselves? Not much to go on here but a gut feeling, yet at the same time the two entity theory seems to make sense, especially when you consider that there's two of virtually everything else on LOST.

Of course the possibility also exists that there's only one monster, but it looks different to everyone who sees it. If this is the case, each individual character would have his or her own perception of what it looks like. What Locke saw in the jungle would be very different from what Eko perceived the monster to look like, and that explanation gels nicely with the perception theory discussed later on in this book.

Red... The Third Grand Master

Another color that can't be ignored is red. It shows up less frequently, but in a more important capacity. When we first meet Mikhail at the Flame Station, we're given hints of a third player as he makes mention of "three grand masters." If LOST is a big game with the characters being used as game pieces, maybe Locke's dead wrong about there only being two players.

Taking the game dynamic a little more literally, we could assume the white pieces are being controlled by one player and the black pieces controlled by an opponent. There are times however, when we see evidence of red influence. It's a third party that seems to show up throughout the show, most notably visible during the launch of the raft at the end of season one when Jin is wearing white, Sawyer's wearing black, and Michael is wearing red. Later on, we find out that Michael gets manipulated - by both The Others and by the island itself - into doing all kinds of things, from shooting Ana Lucia and Libby to returning on the freighter to play a vital part of that whole scenario. It's almost as if Michael's playing two sides of the game board, at least for a little while. This also lends significance to the seemingly meaningless joke Michael tells his nurse in *Special*: "What's black and white and red all over?" Maybe the answer is *him*.

Benjamin Linus is another character that's walked both sides of the fence, even when he didn't know it. His kitchen is black and white, but with a solid red backsplash. If red is the color that represents a third player, or third possibility, maybe that's why the Swan timer's warning hieroglyphics contain red characters in contrast to the black and white numbers of the countdown clock. Maybe when we see red, we're seeing influence from a third party - someone or something not associated with the cut and dry duality of the rest of the show.

Just seeing the color red appear by itself may not mean anything at all, but when it shows up alongside its black and white counterparts we're getting an intentional glimpse of a third side. As Locke rolls up his father's driveway in *Deus Ex Machina* there's a black car, a white car, and Locke driving a bright red VW bug. We know for a fact that Locke is probably the most manipulated of all our main characters, and his puppetry continues both off-island and on. Maybe the shiny red color of his car denotes an outside influence from forces we haven't even seen yet.

Science and Faith... Free Will and Fate

Mirroring the outward struggles of good and evil, LOST also deals with the inner battles between science and faith. In season one we watched a show about a bunch of survivors trying to get rescued after a plane crash, but by that season's finale we realized we were into something much deeper. Similarly, characters like Jack who were slow to accept the island's miracles held strong stances on what was possible and impossible, while champions of faith - Locke for instance - worked on converting them into believing otherwise.

A big moment comes in *Orientation*, where Locke convinces Jack that he needs to be the first person to push the Swan timer button. "You do it, Jack", he tells him. "You have to do it. It's a leap of faith." And with one second left on the clock Jack finally hits the button, his internal pendulum swinging in the direction of faith for the first time since arriving on the island. This is the first in a long chain of events that finally turns Jack from a man of science into, several seasons later, a man who begins to believe in something a lot more unsubstantial.

As it became obvious to the Flight 815 survivors that they were dealing with some undeniably crazy stuff, even those offering the most staunch resistance had to give up their position. In time even they had to admit that, on the island at least, science played little part in things. Faith ruled, and it also rewarded. John Locke's legs were a gift granted him by the island under the condition that he remain faithful, but the very second he started to doubt its motives in *Deus Ex Machina*, the island took the ability to walk right back from him. Along the same lines, Rose's faith that Bernard was alive could be the very reason they had a reunion at all.

By seasons two and beyond however, the battle between science and faith further evolved into something else: free will vs. fate. The writers bludgeoned us over and over with huge clues on this one, starting with the strange set of rules The Others seemed to abide by. As we learned more and more about the island's native protectors, we found out there were things they just couldn't do. More specifically, for all their power and total control over the island, they still seemed unable to *make* anyone do anything.

In *Three Minutes*, Ms. Klugh tells Michael he needs to help them secure the release of Ben. When he asks why The Others don't just march into the 815er's camp and rescue him, she tells him "We can't do that." She goes on to give him specific instructions to bring four people back with him: Jack, Kate, Sawyer and Hurley... three of which The Others had already captured not too long ago in *The Hunting Party*. So what's changed? Why do The Others suddenly need Jack, Kate, and Sawyer when they'd already had them surrounded at gunpoint? Perhaps the answer lies in the issue of free will: The Others couldn't take them the first time around because they need these characters to come *freely*, all on their own accord.

Some of the best evidence of this theory occurs during *The*

Cost of Living, where Ben explains the long con he was trying to use in order to get Jack to perform his spinal surgery. He tells Jack his plan was to "Get you to trust us. And then of course we'd lead you to believe that you were choosing to do...whatever we asked you to do. All of this of course assumed that you would get... invested." When Jack finally realizes Ben's intentions, he asks "You want me to save your life?" To which Ben replies, "No, I want you to *want* to save my life."

As far as how the island works in terms of faith and hope, there appears to be a huge difference between getting someone to do something, and getting them to *want* to do it. Ben uses the word 'invested' here because there's no other easy way to explain it. It's likely that if Jack hadn't needed Ben's surgery to go well, he probably would've died on the table. As with everything else Jack's touched during his lifetime - going all the way back to repairing Sarah's own impossibly damaged spine - Ben knows that Jack's success rate is directly proportional to his belief in succeeding. Ben can't force Jack to do anything because the island simply doesn't work that way, which is why he needs Jack to *choose* to do the operation of his own free will.

Ben however, is a master illusionist. In the game of LOST he bends the rules almost to the breaking point, yet still staying within the scope of his Book of Laws. If the island were a giant pinball machine, Benjamin Linus knows exactly how much he can tip things in his favor before causing it to TILT.

The fact that he manipulates Kate and Sawyer's situation in order to strong-arm Jack into choosing to operate could be described as borderline cheating... but all throughout the show this is traditionally Ben's way of getting people to do things. Alex even tells this to Locke in *The Man From Tallahassee*: "That's what my father does. He manipulates people. He makes you think it's your idea, but it's his."

It also seems that free will plays a huge part in how LOST's overall game plays out. No matter who the two (or three) major players turn out to be, it seems they only have partial control over the playing pieces. Black and white aren't necessarily cut and dry, and sometimes we see evidence of a piece switching sides, or colors. This happens often throughout the show, in the form of internal manipulation as well as part of natural character development. As Jack turns from a man of science into a man of faith, Sawyer goes from bad guy to good. And as Ben goes from sinister leader of the Others to sharing a candy bar with Hurley, we could make the assumption that although each player controls a side, he doesn't have complete control over any of the pieces. Not as long as free will exists, at any rate.

Leaping back again to Jacob and his opponent, it would seem that each of them must abide by whatever choices the characters make. However, they also seem to have their own set of methods for manipulating free will. In some situations, you could even say that free will is twisted into a pre-determined fate, all by convincing the characters of LOST that no matter what they choose to do, the outcome of their actions has already been decided.

Take Ms. Hawking for example. She intentionally meets up with Desmond to convince him that he's got no shot at making a life for himself, and that he needs to return to the island. In season five, she also guides her son Daniel on his own path of "destiny", even though she knows it leads to his death. She's a firm believer that things need to play out a certain way, and that free will has no part in the end game. At the same time however, it's somehow her responsibility to manipulate people despite her belief in fate. She guides them into doing her bidding by letting them *think* they're making their own choices. She tweaks the game board a little, as she does in showing Desmond the red-shoed man who gets killed outside her shop. Ultimately though, the final decisions on what to do seem to lie within the characters themselves.

Some of these game pieces actually rebel against this manipulation, shunning the idea of a predetermined fate. "Don't tell me what I can't do" is a common theme, and a variation of this phrase is uttered by almost every major character in the show at one point or another. Desmond alters the natural course of fate by saving Charlie's life numerous times, despite the island's attempts to course-correct him dead again. And Hurley takes an even tougher and more comical stance against not being able to change destiny by attempting to rewrite *The Empire Strikes Back*.

Benjamin Linus and Charles Widmore

As the game references piled up throughout the show, we as viewers began choosing up our own sides. By seasons three and four, Linus vs. Widmore was a landslide favorite when it came to who was playing against whom. It seemed these two epic characters were pitted against one another for a much longer time than we'd been shown so far, eternally battling for control of the island. It also appeared they were both bound by the same Book of Laws when it came to allowing free choices, at least until Charles Widmore seemingly broke these rules in *The Shape of Things To Come.*

It's here that Ben gets his first taste of a flagrant foul. When his daughter Alex is killed in cold blood by Martin Keamy, Ben is absolutely convinced that Widmore violated or "changed" the rules. Later on when he faces Keamy, his first question is one that's extremely important to him: "Did Charles Widmore *tell* you to kill my daughter?" Ben knows that Widmore, playing by the same set of laws, wouldn't (or shouldn't) be allowed to directly order the execution of his daughter. But if Keamy murdered Alex by his own hand, of his own free will? Then maybe Widmore found his own little loophole. Just as Ben traditionally sets up situations in which characters do his bidding by making their own choices, it seems that Widmore may have done the same thing by hiring the biggest programmable robot of a heartless mercenary he could find. In Ben's eyes, Widmore is still responsible. He knew full well that Keamy would kill his daughter without having to tell him to do so.

Charles however, sees things a bit differently. He puts the blame on Ben for Alex's death. In his eyes, Alex should've died all those years ago when Charles ordered both her and her mother killed. By disobeying him and bringing the baby back alive, Ben was disobeying the very will of the island itself. Charles tells him this years earlier in *Dead is Dead*, claiming that "if the island wants her (Alex) dead, she'll be dead." If Alex was supposed to die as an infant, the act of Ben saving and raising her as his own was only delaying her death. "You cannot fight the inevitable", Widmore tells him, right before being banished from the island. When looked at from this perspective, Alex's death wasn't breaking the rules at all - by indirectly causing her death, Charles was merely carrying out the original will of the island.

Regardless of who's right or wrong, one thing remains the same: there are some rules that cannot be broken. As Ben enters Widmore's bedroom, Charles asks "Have you come here to kill me, Benjamin?" to which Ben replies, "We both know I can't do that." This situation is exactly mirrored at the end of season five. Jacob's nemesis expresses an overwhelming desire to kill him, but for unknown reasons he can't do it directly. He needs to find a loophole if he wants Jacob dead; the game they're playing involves the manipulation and control of outside forces that *can* be used to harm one another... so long as they both stay within the general scope of the island's law.

Jacob and His Dark-Shirted Nemesis

LOST's most recent pair of opponents is handed to us during the season five finale, in probably one of the most important scenes of the entire show. We finally get to see Jacob, who seems like a pretty easy-going guy compared to the shadowy cabin apparitions we've been shown in the past. His antagonist is equally placid, and their conversation seems pretty mundane for a little while. Eventually though, the dark-shirted man can't mask his disdain for Jacob any longer. Once again he's been dragged out of the jungle - forced to deal with yet another group of people Jacob has summoned to the island. We get the impression of a long, seemingly endless game being played - one that Jacob's adversary is getting very tired of being forced to take part in.

Defining the two opposing sides, Jacob seems to champion free will while his competition embraces fate - at first glance, anyway. The most compelling evidence of this occurs during Jacob's cab ride with Hurley during *The Incident*. Of all the main characters Jacob visits this episode, the conversation he has with Hugo seems the most important. In mentioning the Ajira airways flight that will take him back to the island, he tells him, "It's your choice, Hugo. You don't have to do anything you don't want to."

The idea of a game with dynamic playing pieces is pretty

unique. Here you've got two players that are allowed to nudge each other's pieces, but not make solid moves with them. Both Jacob and his adversary become the architects of a very long and complicated series of events, each designed to manipulate certain characters into doing what they want. From beginning to end, we see characters that are guided by what they perceive to be the island's will, and other characters who act almost upon direct orders.

In *The Incident*, Jacob identifies pieces he's going to be playing with even as early as the childhood of some of the main characters. Years before the crash of Flight 815 we see him visiting Kate and Sawyer during their youth, and Sun, Jin, Locke, Sayid and Jack during adulthood. He shows up at what appear to be critical moments in these characters' lives, physically touching the game pieces as if marking them in some way. Later on when these people finally get to the island, Jacob is already invested in them - John Locke in particular.

And if you buy into the theory of two monsters, you could make the argument that Jacob's enemy takes the form of one - the black smoke perhaps - while he himself takes several forms as another. In *This Place is Death*, there's a scene where ghost-Christian convinces Locke that he needs to turn the frozen donkey wheel. He also gives very specific orders on how to bring the Oceanic Six back to the island. But when Locke asks for something as simple as help standing up? Christian tells him "No. Sorry, I can't." His inability to directly interfere is consistent with the "rules", so to speak. This is why Dave couldn't push Hurley off that cliff, or why Ms. Hawking couldn't throw shackles around Desmond and ship him off to the island... each person has to make his or her own choices in LOST. That's not to say the players of the game can't take the ink out of Claire's pen, or jam the gun Michael tries to shoot himself with, but affecting things directly seems to be prohibited.

In fact, we're forced to wonder how far back the game really goes - especially considering what we've seen of Jacob. Just how many moves ahead do the players have mapped out? "Everything happens for a reason" takes on a whole new meaning when you throw away sheer coincidence and apply some past engineering by a pair of ageless, all-powerful demigods. Did John Locke's kidney get swiped because Cooper conned him, or because someone knew that sometime in his future, a bullet would pass through the left side of his body? Was Jack brought to the island because one player knew the other would eventually give Ben a spinal tumor? Was Charlie brought in specifically to play *Good Vibrations* in The Looking Glass station? So many moves seem to have countermoves, it's no wonder so many of LOST's themes are often seen mirrored and backwards.

Did Jacob's opponent allow the freighter to find the island, permitting the Oceanic six to escape? Was it Jacob's countermove in sending Locke to bring them back? And when Locke did return - this time in a coffin - did the dark-shirted man not only anticipate that this would happen, but actually *rely* upon it so that he could take Locke's form? Looking at things from such an angle, this series of events allowed the dark man to con Richard into bringing him right to Jacob's doorstep. And along the way, he was mentally and emotionally honing his weapon - a very dejected Benjamin Linus - to a razor sharp edge. Not able to kill Jacob directly, the dark man supplied the anger, motivation, and even the knife that plunges into Jacob's heart... pulling off what could be LOST's longest con of all.

But is there an even longer con, perpetuated by Jacob? Although we've seen his death, I don't think we've seen the end of the adjustments he's made to LOST's game board. It's very possible that his enemy's seemingly well-laid plans might fall within the scope of Jacob's own secret agenda. Based upon how long they've been playing (and more specifically, how Jacob virtually goaded Ben into stabbing him), I'm betting that he's still got an ace up his sleeve. I'm also convinced that free will is destined to win out over predetermination. That's just my opinion of course, but overall I think it makes for a more interesting ending.

Everything Changes vs. Whatever Happened, Happened

Jin was the first to say it, standing next to a creepy-looking guy in a chicken suit way back in *Everybody Hates Hugo*. "Everything is going to change", he tells Hurley, and in flawless English to boot. The island's way of getting this message across might seem pretty bizarre at first glance, but choosing to dress the vendor of Hurley's winning lotto ticket in a Mr. Cluck's suit was an appeal directly to him. These references were made because they were either pulled from Hugo's mind, or because they were memories the island knew he would quickly identify with. And of all the Flight 815 survivors the island could've used to deliver the message, choosing a non-English speaking character was just another way of attaching more significance to the announcement.

On the flip side of Everything's Going to Change, we have Everything Happens for a Reason. These two schools of thought end up dividing the characters into two very opposite camps by the time season four rolls around. John Locke ends up as the poster boy for faith, but a twisted, darker version of faith that seems to indicate that nothing in the future can be changed. He stomps through the jungles of LOST trying to figure out what's "supposed to" be done, trusting blindly in the randomly intermittent orders the island keeps giving him. We know just how serious he is when we watch him throw a knife into Naomi's back during the season three finale, and it soon becomes obvious that - like Ben and The Others - Locke will stop at nothing to accomplish the island's goals.

When full-blown time travel is sprung upon us in season five, we get a first-hand look at how the forces of destiny seem to work. As the island phases in and out of various points in its own history, the main characters travel with it. Yet no matter what they do or how hard they try, everything seems to have little or no impact on the future they've already seen. In some cases it even turns out that traveling backward through time is actually *necessary* to the storylines we've watched in the past four seasons of LOST. The actions of our past-dwelling heroes account for many of the life-changing events they've already experienced, brought full circle by the contact they make in their own pasts. Daniel Faraday actually ends up being the "crazy man" Charlotte remembers from her childhood, as described during *This Place is Death*. We also find out that Miles has an even stronger and more influential role in his own destiny. Warning his father of the impending disaster about to befall Dharma, Miles becomes responsible for his own bastardization when Dr. Chang ends up sending his wife and child - who turns out to be Miles himself as a baby - away from the island, never to see them again.

The argument of whether or not the past can be altered to affect a seemingly established future is carried on between Jacob and his nemesis in their conversation on the beach. The dark-shirted man asserts that things "always end the same", arguing that people are just too violent and corrupt to ever be able to change anything. Jacob however, believes in change. He points out to his adversary that there's really only one ending. In his eyes, "Anything that happens before that is just progress", which seems to indicate that ultimately, he believes there will be a different and unique outcome to the ever-looping sequence of events that seem to make up LOST's universe.

While both sides of the argument have merit, one of the flaws in the predetermination camp seems to be the fact that destiny on LOST is not always set in stone. In fact, it's often fabricated by a large network of people struggling very hard to make sure that whatever happened actually *did* happen. Eloise Hawking is one of these agents, and her plate is pretty full. Besides appearing before Desmond in the ring shop, Eloise is also tasked with the pretty big workload of making sure the Oceanic Six get back to the island. We find out her responsibilities also include shaping and molding her son Daniel's future for the interests of the island. She shuts down Faraday's career as a pianist, stomps out his social life, builds him up academically and strips away any chance at keeping a girlfriend... all so later on down the road she can knowingly and tearfully sacrifice him for the greater good.

But hey, why does destiny need a babysitter at all? The very definition of Whatever Happened, Happened seems to indicate that the outcome of everything is already predetermined. If that's the case, why is there a whole network of people working for Benjamin Linus, both on and off the island, striving to keep things "happening" a certain way? As Ben flies all over the world plotting and scheming, there are times he sure seems worried that things won't fall into place. In *The Lie*, he even tells Jill the butcher: "If you don't (keep

Locke safe)... everything we're about to do won't matter at all." These aren't the words of someone convinced that everything is ruled by fate. In fact, all the work Ben and The Others seem to be doing for the past five seasons might actually be geared to *counter* the idea that the future is set in stone. In working for the island, perhaps these game pieces are really being manipulated to reverse the idea of fate - to oppose the effects of course-correction - all the while believing that they're working toward achieving some predetermined destiny.

In one of the coolest scenes of season five, Miles and Hurley spend several minutes debating the fate vs. free will argument. Miles hands out a lot of good evidence that the future can't be changed; no matter what they do they're only going through the preprogrammed motions of a destiny already etched in stone. Every move they make is nothing but an illusion of free will... while they believe they're making their own choices, the path they follow has already been predetermined. Hugo however, refuses to accept fate this easily. He even tries to work around it in *Some Like it Hoth*, and as comical as his new screenplay might seem, the fact that it's being rewritten by Hurley is symbolically important. In another theory you'll read about later on in this book, there's a mountain of evidence pointing to the fact that maybe Hurley *can* change things.

The situation is probably best explained best by Daniel Faraday in *Because You Left*. He tells Sawyer, "Time is like a street. We can move forward on that street, we can move in reverse, but we cannot ever create a new street. If we try to do anything different, we will fail every time. Whatever happened, happened." Later on however, Dan changes his tune. "I forgot about the variables", he tells Jack. "Us. We're the variables. People. We think. We reason. We make choices. We have free will. We can change our destiny." This little speech is important, because it actually convinces Jack to carry out Daniel's plan to detonate Jughead even after Faraday is killed. This leaves us wondering if Hawking really sent Daniel back to die for nothing, or if she somehow knew he'd plant the seeds that would get the bomb detonated. A third option exists also: one of the game's *players* knew everything would happen this way, manipulating both Hawking and Daniel without their knowledge. Breaking it down like that, you could apply this principal to the entire show.

The culmination of the destiny vs. change argument occurs at the end of *The Incident*, where Juliet hammers Jughead's nuclear core with (of all things) a black rock. On her eighth hit we're slammed with LOST's closing logo, but for the first time ever we're shown a negative image of it. Black and white are reversed, which could mean that the bomb went off and some major changes in the storyline have occurred. As explained earlier in the show, small changes in history can always be course-corrected... but a change as big as a nuclear explosion might jar loose a whole new timeline where anything goes.

While it looks like we're going to find out very early on in season six whether or not change has occurred, I think the end result will be a lot less cut and dry than most people might think. Going back to LOST's roots we can't just forget about the recurring themes of faith, belief, and even suggestive manifestation. This isn't a show about time travel or temporal physics - it goes much, much deeper than that. Whether or not Jughead detonated might well depend on how much our characters *believe* it went off. By the time Jack drops the bomb down that shaft, he, Kate, Sawyer, and even Juliet are all beginning to get convinced that their plan will work. Maybe they're convincing themselves out of necessity or even self-preservation, but most of them are starting to actually *will* this change to happen. They're all so sick of being on the island, they actually *need* for their plan to work. Could their combined efforts force a new timeline? Maybe one of them believing in the plan isn't enough, but all of their faith combined together is what creates an impact?

In any case, *The Incident* becomes one of the biggest moves on the chessboard of LOST. It's an event preceded by a dozen other moves, all of them designed to get these characters together at that one particular place, at that one particular moment in time. We might find out the result is nothing more than what was "supposed" to happen, or we may find that the game board itself has been radically changed. No matter what happens though, it's no lucky accident that the dark man's apparent victory over Jacob seems to run parallel to the 1977 timeline's climax at the Swan site. Each of these players have been planning ahead, but it's the one who gains the final move who will end up winning the game.

Exiting or Being Removed From The Game

If LOST does turn out to be one big game, the capture and removal of the game pieces is an all-important aspect. Since season one we've seen death on the island, but we've also seen rebirth and resurrection. Just as chess pieces can return to the game board during a heated match (and coming back with more power than ever), we've watched "dead" characters return as apparitions (Charlie, Ana Lucia), in dream sequences (Boone, Horace), and also as forms of the smoke monster (Christian, Yemi, Libby, Alex, and perhaps even John Locke). We've also seen people we thought were dead show up again unexpectedly, like Mikhail.

Death never seemed final on LOST, even before the time travel aspect of the show brought back many of characters who'd already kicked the bucket. Many of the actual deaths themselves were a bit suspect as well. According to Locke in *Exodus Part 2*, Boone's death was "a sacrifice the island demanded." Charlie seemed to be killed off as part of the island trying to course correct Desmond's attempts to save him. These facts are all pretty important, but what's really interesting are the words spoken by these characters *after* they're dead... and sometimes even just before.

Once again, we need to examine Boone's last words to Jack. As Jack tries to convince him that amputation is the only real chance of saving his life, Boone tells him, "There's no chance. Really. I mean, *look where we are*." Shortly before dying

Boone takes on a resigned, almost exhausted disposition. Yes he's in physical pain and he's lost a lot of blood... but he's emotionally tired, too. As he lets Jack off the hook on his promise to save him, Boone's giving up and passing over to that "other side" we so often hear about during the show. And just before he leaves, Boone seems to suddenly *know* something... as if he's getting a glimpse of where the Flight 815 survivors really, truly are.

Now take the death of Ana Lucia. On the surface, Michael shooting her point blank in the midsection during *Two For The Road* seems to come as a pretty big surprise, both to her and to us. But as friend and fellow ODI podcaster of mine Karen (from *karenslostnotebook.blogspot.com*) points out, you don't even need the episode title to see this exit coming. Ana Lucia is physically and emotionally drained. Rewatching the scene with her sitting on the couch, she looks completely and utterly exhausted. Some of her last words to Michael, right before dying? "I can't do this anymore."

So is Ana's departure self-induced? Is she taking herself out of the game voluntarily? More evidence exists a scene earlier, where she's calling her mother from Sidney, Australia. In a scene not unlike Trinity calling Morphius to take her out of *The Matrix*, Ana Lucia is telling her mother "I want to come home." She explains that she got as far away as she could, but now she's finally finished running and wants to return. A few minutes later Ana is removed from the island by the hand of Michael.

But if you watch that scene again, you'll notice something else very interesting: Michael himself is surprised. In killing Ana Lucia and Libby, he seems to have acted impulsively and without orders. Later on during *Meet Kevin Johnson*, he tries to pin the blame for the murders on Benjamin Linus. Ben however, won't have any of it. He absolves himself of the innocent blood, responding with "You killed them, Michael. No one asked you to." Considering the ghostly appearance of Christian right before Michael's death a few episodes later, we find out Ben might just be wrong about that. Someone or some*thing* might've forced Michael's hand - another nudge of the game board's playing pieces to get a certain job done.

Examining the demise of Charlie, we see him knowingly embrace his own death as sacrifice in *Through The Looking Glass*. After having fought so hard to stay alive he finally lets go, hoping that dying will somehow save Claire and Aaron from the island. The manner of his death is even foreshadowed way back in season one, where he's singing "Itsy Bitsy Spider" to Aaron in *The Greater Good*. Charlie gets every line of the nursery rhyme correct, except when he says "Down came the rain and *drowned* the spider out." Hurley even calls him on the error and makes the correction. Two seasons later Charlie drowns; an eerie coincidence, or just another example of how far ahead the players have mapped out their moves in the game of LOST.

Another pretty big clue that the characters can remove themselves from the game occurs during *Maternity Leave*. In the long corridor of the Staff station, where Ethan took Claire to have her baby, there's a small door set into the right-side wall. Above it, the door is labeled: "Escape Hatch." Is this a quick exit put there by Dharma in case they needed to abandon the station quickly? Or is it another subtle message that the characters can stop playing at any time simply by opting out?

Visits From Beyond The Game... and Grave

At times, still-living characters seem to receive sudden visits from those characters who have passed on or gone over to the other side. Jack is visited by his dad, Eko by his brother, Michael by the ghost of Libby. Locke sees Boone in a startling vision, and Ben sees his daughter Alex. But you know what these visits have in common? For all of them, you can make a case that each of these characters were somehow responsible for the death of the person visiting them from beyond the grave. Jack reporting his father's alcoholism sent Christian into a downward spiral from which he never recovered. Eko was almost directly responsible for his brother getting shot. Michael killed Libby outright, Locke unknowingly sacrificed Boone to the island, and Ben's refusal to surrender resulted in Keamy killing Alex. In a way, you could say these characters are all being visited by manifestations of their own guilty conscience.

There is one exception however: Hugo Reyes. For reasons unknown, Hurley's role as a ghost-magnet doesn't seem to discriminate. He's been visited by Charlie and Ana Lucia after they've died, both of whom made attempts to guide him back to the island. Hugo has also played chess with the ghost of Mr. Eko, and appears to be one of the only people with the ability to see Jacob's cabin. Off-island, even the living characters go out of their way to visit him, important ones like Jack, Locke, Jacob, Abaddon and Walt. Someone always seems to be keeping an eye on Hurley, even at the Santa Rosa mental health facility. Overall, Hugo's situation seems rather unique.

Influencing The Game From The Outside

Some of the most tantalizing moments in LOST have occurred during the return of dead characters, where we're given an almost direct glimpse of what's "really going on." When Charlie showed up to visit Hurley in the season four premiere episode *The Beginning of The End*, his appearance was devoid of the ghostly, dreamlike qualities we'd so often seen in past flashbacks or visions. No, this time Charlie seemed real - so real in fact, that Hurley's fellow mental patient Lewis can even point him out. And as Charlie sat down to talk to Hurley many of us bolted upright to the edge of our seats, hoping that some very big answers to some very big questions were finally about to be revealed.

What's strange about ghost-Charlie's appearance in this episode is how very much in character he stays. He works hard to convince Hurley that he's truly there while still admitting to being dead. Having been a major character throughout the entire show, we know a lot about Charlie's personality. Watching him treat Hurley with kid gloves while still trying to deliver his message was consistent with his compassion, but at the same time Charlie also demonstrated a behavior he simply didn't have while alive on the island: restraint.

Charlie *knows* something. As he cryptically tells Hurley "They need you", he refrains from telling him why. He doesn't explain to his friend how he can be dead and yet still be talking to him, and doesn't give Hurley any direct answers. On the contrary, the Charlie of the past three seasons was a character who eternally chased after those answers. Whenever something inexplicable happened, he demanded to know how and why. Charlie was the first one throwing his arms up in protest at the island's craziest moments, even as other people seemed to accept the strangest of circumstances. Yet now here he is, talking directly to Hurley, able to give his friend (and us) *all* of the answers to *all* of the questions... and yet he doesn't. Instead, Charlie gives Hurley nothing but a simple nudge. He knows his friend well enough to press his emotional guilt buttons, pushing Hugo into doing what somehow needs to be done.

And just as we're achingly close to getting a peek behind the big curtain, Hugo closes his eyes and counts to five. When he opens them again, his buddy is gone. But the very fact that Charlie doesn't tell Hurley anything important actually tells us quite a lot. It reiterates a very recurring and important LOST rule: the people still stuck within the game aren't *allowed* to know why. Charlie doesn't tell Hurley what's really going on not because he doesn't know, but because he isn't permitted to give him that kind of information. And if a character like Charlie is withholding this kind of knowledge from his closest friend, then there has to be a pretty good reason for it.

In *Further Instructions*, we see more evidence of controlled outside influence. Locke actually communes with the island so he can find out what to do next, and a vision of Boone is given to him for guidance. As if to pointedly remind Locke of the price of failure, Boone immediately puts Locke back into his wheelchair. An argument could be made that this vision of Boone isn't really Boone at all, but more of doppleganger who appears to John in a familiar form. But then Boone mentions being "the sacrifice the island demanded", sardonically throwing Locke's words right back into his face. For a moment we get a glimpse of the old Boone - the one who questioned Locke about the futility of trying to open the hatch.

As he wheels John through the Sydney Airport, Boone drops hints about specific areas of LOST's storyline, character by character. He obviously has advanced knowledge of what's going to happen, claiming that Charlie, Claire and Aaron will be "fine... for a while", before pointing out Jack, Kate, and Sawyer and telling John, "There's nothing you can do for them. Not yet." The only real answer he gives Locke is that he needs to help Mr. Eko, who as it turns out was somehow dragged into a cave by a giant CGI polar bear. Again we have someone who's dead or gone influencing the game from the outside, but not really able to provide a detailed plan or definitive answers.

Boone's inability to directly interfere is vocalized when he tells John "You have to clean up your own mess." These are the same words Benjamin Linus would use on Locke later on when Anthony Cooper, "The Man from Tallahassee", makes a surprise appearance on the island. Mistakenly thinking that Cooper is there as a direct result of Locke's own daddy issues, Ben orders John to kill him. When Locke asks why The Others can't just bring him along as a prisoner, Ben perpetuates the theme of being powerless to intercede by responding with "He's your mess, John. Why would we clean it up?"

But putting aside all the characters who are dead and gone, we also see outside influence from two characters who haven't even died yet - not that we know of, anyway. These characters happen to appear at a very critical moment during one of LOST's most important episodes, and indirectly, they even try to talk other characters out of certain courses of action. The episode I'm talking about is *The Incident*, and the characters I'm referring to are Rose and Bernard... two characters who, at the time we see them, seem to have removed *themselves* from the game.

If you haven't done so already, go back and take a really good look at this scene again. Sawyer, Kate and Juliet stumble across Vincent (this fact alone should make us wary), who then leads them to some very castaway-like versions of Rose and

Bernard. Somehow they've been living undetected in the jungle for several years, in a dwelling that looks suspiciously like Jacob's cabin. Is this more of the island's repeat manufacturing? Maybe. But the important thing here is how Rose and Bernard treat our main characters as they stop at their little sanctuary in the middle of nowhere.

As Sawyer asks why his fellow crash survivors didn't approach him for Dharma recruitment, we get Rose's very telling answer: "Because we're retired." Bernard goes on to explain how they're now living in peace, down by the ocean, in a place "we've made for ourselves" - an interesting choice of words if you consider the on-island manifestation of people's wants, needs, and desires. When Sawyer and Kate talk about a bomb, Rose responds with "Who cares?" And when an incredulous Kate can't understand why she's so unconcerned, Rose tells her "It's always something with *you people*."

Now you can take this scene at face value, and believe that an old married couple is just making the best of a bad situation. Or if you really want answers, you can dive a little deeper into what's truly going on.

The Rose and Bernard we see during *The Incident* are clearly living outside the realm of LOST's play field. They've checked out, so to speak, and are no longer a part of the overall game. Rose's use of the word "retired" is well-placed, because they're no longer a part of the actual storyline. Somehow they've figured out how the island works; they've broken the code, unraveled the mystery, and solved the riddle. They don't have to worry about food, water, time travel, the smoke monster, Rose's cancer, or anything else anymore. As Rose puts it, the two of them suddenly realized that they've got "everything that people try their whole lives" to obtain, sitting right smack in front of them the entire time.

The very moment these characters came to this realization may be the moment they achieved true enlightenment, allowing them to finally "leave." This is similar to a concept once explained in detail by Damon Lindelof: "This show is about people who are metaphorically lost in their lives, who get on an airplane, and crash on an island, and become physically lost on the planet Earth. And once they are able to metaphorically find themselves in their lives again, they will be able to physically find themselves in the world again."

This is akin to saying that once you stop running from all the flaming arrows and pull the plug on trying to set off nuclear bombs - the moment you *embrace* the things that are important to you rather than try and fight against what's not - you're finally given the chance to cross over to that other side. It's almost as if LOST is a big stage, and the actors wake up on it without realizing how they got there. They begin by running through their same old habits, living out the same old patterns, not even knowing they're just playing parts in a show. But once they can break those patterns and truly evolve? It's like each character who does so has stepped into a new area of the stage and sees what was *behind* the curtain. At this point they realize exactly where they are, maybe smack themselves in the forehead for not realizing it sooner, and they step offstage for good. Once out of LOST's multi-act play they cannot go back... but some of them can watch from the sidelines and, at times, perhaps influence or help along those people who are having a hard time figuring things out on their own.

This may be why Bernard actually tries to stop Juliet from leaving in this scene. As she walks away to what looks to be certain death, he asks "You sure you don't want some tea?" Bernard's look of sadness when she refuses, coupled with Juliet's hand resting on her stomach, have led viewers to speculate that she's pregnant with Sawyer's baby. Whether she is or not, Bernard *knows* what's going to happen next. He's obviously unable to tell his friends directly, but he is allowed to at least give Juliet the choice to stay. Her making the right decision was a long shot at best, but Bernard felt he had to try.

The Whispers - Voices From The Outside Looking In

It's one of LOST's oldest-standing mysteries and one that ultimately demands some type of explanation: the whispers in the jungle. Since Sayid first began hearing them outside Danielle's house in season one, some of the more major events in the storyline have been accompanied by eerie, hurried whispers from unknown places. They're usually so low that they need to be enhanced in order to be properly heard. Some of them are layered, with several audio tracks playing simultaneously. Still other whispers are reversed, or in different languages. And since the beginning, dedicated LOST fans have gone to great lengths to find out exactly what's being said by these hidden watchers in the jungle... if they're really in the jungle at all.

We know two definite facts about the whispers. First, they're non-corporeal. It's not like a bunch of people are crouched in the bushes just out of sight, whispering to the 815 crash survivors. Second, they're intelligent to the current situation; the comments made by the whisperers seem to pertain to what's going on in that particular scene or episode. It's as if a group of people are watching what's going on and commenting on it to each other, on some frequency too low or fast to be deciphered by the characters participating in the story.

One of the easiest conclusions to jump to about the whispers is that they consist of the ghostly voices of our dead characters. There's a lot of evidence pointing to this, starting with Frank Duckett's voice distinctly echoing "It'll come back around." Even more convincingly this occurs during *Outlaws*, a Sawyer-centric episode in which Frank is murdered. We also hear what sounds a lot like Boone's voice within the whispers during *Abandoned*, just before Shannon is killed by Ana Lucia. The words "Hi sis" certainly seem to fit. "Shannon, meet me on the other side" is an even stronger indication that what we're hearing aren't just echoes from the past, but actual voices from people who are watching the current storyline unfold. "Dying sucks", also whispered in Boone's voice, makes reference to the fact that he's already experienced death by that point.

In *A Tale of Two Cities*, Jack starts hearing the whispers from what Juliet tells him is a broken intercom. Transcripts from that exchange reveal Christian Shephard's voice telling him "Let it go, Jack." We already know Jack has trouble letting go, because his father tells him the exact same thing in *Do No Harm*. Young Benjamin Linus also hears his dead mother's voice in *The Man Behind The Curtain*, telling him "It's alright. It's okay." Both Ben and Jack have physically seen a deceased parent on the island too, but despite chasing after them haven't been able to catch up.

There are a variety of other voices within the whispers also, but the quality leaves them open to interpretation. The translation of what one person hears might be different from the next. Some people claim that it's Hurley's voice saying "Relax dude", within the whispers in *The Other 48 Days*. This contradicts the theory that the voices belong solely to the ghosts of dead characters, but still doesn't rule out the idea that the whispers are being created by people on the outside looking in. For one reason or another, the characters on the island are being secretly observed and commented on.

And in some cases, individual characters within the whispers themselves seem to want to help. In the very first whispers we hear during *Solitary*, a woman's voice suggests actually talking to Sayid. "Could just speak to him", she says, but she's immediately overruled by a man's voice saying "No." In *Outlaws*, perhaps the same woman's voice is heard again, suggesting this time that they speak to Sawyer. "Maybe we should just talk to him?" she offers. Once again a man's voice overrides the idea, quickly saying "No, if he sees us it will ruin everything."

Throughout many episodes the whispers attempt to hush each other, indicating they know it's possible that the characters can hear them. They also talk about hurrying up, hiding, and being quiet. At one point the whispers talk about using the characters to "help" them, but there doesn't yet seem to be enough trust. Whatever the voices may be trying to accomplish, if anything, for now it seems they do little but watch as the game unfolds.

The Watchers - Spectators of the Game

Another one of the more common themes of the show can be summed up in a single word: *watching*. There's an exceptional amount of watching that happens on the island, starting with the Dharma Initiative's Pearl Station monitors and continuing on to Ben watching the Hydra cages and Jack's cell from his control room. During *The Life and Death of Jeremy Bentham*, Charles Widmore admits to Locke that he's been watching the O6, citing that he's deeply invested in the future of the island. Later in the same episode, Ben tells Locke the same thing: "I have a man watching Sayid. I'm watching *all* of them (the O6), keeping them safe." And in a reverse of that same situation, once Ben returns to the island Caesar tells him that Locke was "watching over him" while he was out cold in *Dead is Dead.*

But the most significant (and perhaps most mysterious) example of watching comes in the middle of season three, during *Stranger in a Strange Land.* Jack groggily wakes up in his cage at the beating zoo to none other than Cindy the Flight 815 stewardess. With her are the children Zach and Emma from the tail section, along with a bunch of other clean, well-dressed people milling around and peering oddly into Jack's cage.

Watch this scene again and look at these people carefully. We're not seeing more Others here. No, these are the Flight 815 survivors who either disappeared or were dragged off in the beginning of the show. Fresh and clean, they're dressed for an air-conditioned plane ride... not for a walk in the sweltering jungle. They don't talk either. Instead they mutter to each other strangely, watching as Jack struggles to understand what's going on. He nods to them over Cindy's shoulder in growing frustration, mistaking them for more of Ben's people. "What are you doing here, with *them*?" Jack demands. "I thought you were taken. You were... captured."

Cindy's reaction is one of the most telling few seconds of the whole season: "They're not... ummm... it's not that simple." Cindy was about to tell Jack something very important here: that the people behind her weren't really *with* The Others. Something however, made her stop. Once again we see that forbidden element - a character who knows something but is powerless to tell the whole story. Jack angrily presses on, demanding "What are they doing here, right now? What are you *doing here!*" And Cindy responds even more oddly when she tells him "We're here to watch, Jack."

Something's visually different about this whole scene too. The lighting is way off - it's too bright, but it's shadowy at the same time. As Faraday would say in *Confirmed Dead*, the light "doesn't scatter quite right." The low murmuring of everyone all at once sounds a lot like the cacophony of whispers we're always hearing in the jungle. The children don't speak to Cindy, they whisper. And when Jack asks what everyone is here to "watch", the 815 flight attendant stumbles around clumsily for an answer she can't give. Not to mention the fact that Jack is encountering these people immediately after sleeping or dreaming, giving us yet another reason not to take the scene completely at face value.

So are these people really a part of The Others, shipped over from the main island to watch Juliet's judgement? Or are they watchers from beyond yet another viewing layer - maybe even looking in from behind the curtain? Keep in mind the only other time we see Cindy is when John Locke encounters her during *The Brig*. And in this scene, much like in Jack's, the only person who sees and interacts with her is Locke himself.

As The Others mill around and set up camp all eyes are curiously drawn to John, with Cindy gently explaining that they've been "waiting a long time" for his arrival.

Finally, the whispers themselves make multiple references to viewing or watching LOST's main characters. During *Abandoned*, one of the ghostly voices even uses the phrase "hide the scope." Whether or not there's a physical piece of equipment being used to see them, our characters are definitely being watched. As credited to Karen Degroot in the Pearl orientation video: "careful observation is the only key to true and complete awareness." Maybe someone should've told this to the poor saps vacuum-launching tubes of useless notebooks into the ass-end of the jungle.

Ending the Game - Winners and Losers

The theory that LOST might be nothing more than a big game has many different facets to it. As with most games it would require players, game pieces, a playing field, and maybe even some spectators. We've certainly seen evidence of these things throughout the show, at all different levels of hierarchy. We've seen inferences that the game might go on forever, as well as hints that it might finally be coming to an end. We've watched moves and countermoves, traps in the process of being sprung and others that were skillfully avoided. But like all games, in the end LOST might require that there be a winner and a loser.

Unless of course, it ends in a draw.

There Are Two Monsters on the Island... And John Locke is One of Them

"Let me go. Just let me go. I'll be alright."
- Locke, after being grabbed by the monster, *Exodus Part 2*

"Oh, John, don't you understand? You don't have a father. You were immaculately conceived."
- Emily, *Deus Ex Machina*

"John... Which of these things belong to you already?"
- Richard Alpert, *Cabin Fever*

"Everything's gonna be alright. I'm sorry this happened to you."
- Jacob, after touching Locke, *The Incident*

Of all the encounters we've seen throughout LOST, the ones involving "the monster" have been among the most interesting.

It grabbed our attention as the first supernatural element of the island, and has continued to be enigmatic throughout the show. There was a time we were starving for any glimpse we could get of Smokey, but as time wore on we were shown more and more of it. Yet the more we rewatch the older episodes, the more we need to ask ourselves exactly what it is that we're seeing.

The idea of there being two monsters has already been discussed briefly. What has not been discussed is the idea that one of them physically manifests itself, at times anyway, as John Locke.

Now as far as theories go, this one's pretty far out there. It involves both a light and a dark monster; one of them existing under Jacob's influence and the other being associated with his adversary. To say that Locke *is* the smoke monster would be totally inaccurate - we all know and love the person that John Locke is, and this theory doesn't take away from that. But at the same time we've seen evidence of Locke being moved or manipulated across both sides of the island's playing field. John Locke is quintessentially dichotomic. He's been a leader and a follower, all-knowing and clueless; over the course of five seasons Locke has demonstrated both extreme gullibility and absolute, total control. He's the one chess piece with two fingers on it, and it's just a matter of picking out which times he's been pushed by each of the two opposing sides.

Locke as the Light Monster

It's generally been accepted that the smoke monster has taken on several human and even nonhuman forms. We've seen everyone from a placid Christian Shephard to a very spooky Yemi all the way down to a really pissed off Alex. Assuming there really *are* two monsters or entities, you could make a case that whenever we see Jack's father we're actually seeing the light one. Perhaps associated with Jacob, this entity was responsible for helping the characters find water and shelter way back during *White Rabbit*. With supplies running low, Jack was seeking both of these things when he encountered his dead father in the jungle. Only by following after him did Jack stumble across the cave complex that the characters would live at for much of season one.

But before Jack finds the caves, he chases his father's ghostly image off the edge of a cliff. Christian Shephard dematerializes... and seemingly from out of nowhere John Locke shows up to rescue Jack from certain death. This is an episode after Locke sees the monster in the jungle, and it's also right about when he *really* starts acting strange. Locke tells Jack that he's looked into the eye of the island, and that what he saw was beautiful. He goes on to talk about the island being special, hallucinations becoming reality, and for the first time ever we get the "Everything that happens, happens for a reason" line. His conversation with Jack is strange and cool, and it sets those nicely mysterious undertones that carry on for the rest of the show.

But even at this point Locke simply *knows* too much.

Logically speaking, there's no way he could have such knowledge. We're only four episodes into the show and something's already happened to change him. His contact with the monster - which he would later describe to Mr. Eko as a "beautiful bright light" - has instilled Locke with an inner understanding of many things on the island. But it also seems as if something was *awakened* within him during that encounter... something that just might always have been there. His mother Emily talks about Locke being special even before he reaches the island, telling him "You're part of a design." She also goes on to tell him that he doesn't even have a father, and that he was "immaculately conceived." So either Locke's father isn't really Anthony Cooper at all (and he answers to a *much* higher authority) or his mother's already off her rocker by the time she stalks him down in the parking lot of Toys R Us.

In any case, more evidence of the connection between Locke and the monster occurs during *Walkabout*. This is the episode where Locke encounters the creature, but for some reason denies seeing it when Michael asks him later on. It's also the first episode in which Jack sees the corpse of his father walking around. As Jack chases Christian for the first time, his father walks into a small grove of trees. Jack bounds in, and this is where he loses sight of him. But just as Jack's looking around to see where his father could've possibly gone, there's movement in the trees... and out comes John Locke, dragging a freshly killed boar.

Locke's impossibly strong communion with the island continues throughout the season. He starts giving out sage advice, tosses his compass over his shoulder, and can suddenly predict rain storms down to the very second. In *House of the Rising Sun*, he guides Charlie through trading his heroin to the island in exchange for his guitar. In *The Moth*, he prevents Sayid from triangulating the location of the radio tower by braining him in the back of the head, perpetuating what we'd later realize to be a very Jacob-like agenda: keeping everyone on the island for as long as possible. In Locke's own words, "We're all here for a reason."

In *Hearts and Minds*, Locke materializes out of the jungle so seamlessly that Sayid doesn't even hear him approaching. "Sorry", John tells him. "I'm sneakier than I give myself credit for." Also in that episode, Locke utters a phrase that would later be used twice by Christian Shephard: "You need to let go." He tells this to Boone, just before whipping up a batch of trip-paste that initiates the vision in which Shannon is killed. Within that same vision, Boone even makes reference to Locke as if he had some other true identity: "Do you know who this guy *is*? He's the only one here that has a clue to what's going on." His choice of words there is interesting, to say the least.

Locke also identifies Walt as "different" while talking to Michael in *Special*. After teaching Walt to throw knives by first picturing the end result in his mind, he strangely mentions that Michael's son should be "allowed to realize his potential" while on the island. Several episodes later in *Born to Run*, it's

Walt who identifies Locke's plan to open the hatch after being grabbed on the wrist by him. "Don't open it", he tells John, displaying an ability to either visualize Locke's thoughts or to somehow see what's going to happen next.

But a huge piece of evidence linking Locke even more tightly to an island entity occurs during *Outlaws*. The boar that terrorizes Sawyer all throughout this episode is undoubtedly a form of the monster, as well as being a manifestation of Sawyer's guilt over killing an innocent Frank Duckett. This is more than likely the same creature Kate will later on see as a black horse during *What Kate Did*, and according to Damon Lindelof during the Official LOST Podcast, it even takes the form of the medusa spiders that paralyze Nikki and Paulo.

Getting back to Sawyer's boar, as he and Kate track it through the jungle it ends up ransacking their camp the next morning. Sawyer realizes his food is gone, asking Kate "It ate all our stuff?" to which Kate replies, "Nope. It ate *your* stuff. Mine's fine." Take a look at the next thing that happens: John Locke comes strolling casually out of the jungle... *and he's eating something*. He even sits down and begins telling a story, one about a human (Locke's deceased sister) that seemingly took the form of an animal (a golden retriever).

So is the boar that Sawyer chases in this episode really John Locke? As John tells Kate when she suggests something similar at the end of his story, "That would be silly." But to say there isn't a direct connection between John's appearance and the monster's disappearance would be ignoring some pretty powerful evidence spread out over multiple episodes, and even multiple seasons.

There's even an indication that the darker "smoke" monster recognizes its counterpart, the light entity, within John Locke. Halfway through *The Cost of Living*, an injured Mr. Eko is drinking from a stream. In its reflection, he sees the smoke monster looming above him. As he turns to face it however, the monster is already retreating... it immediately withdraws and darts quickly away. And as Eko turns back around to see what caused it to flee, John Locke comes walking into frame. The smoke monster ran from him, not from Eko.

The question then becomes this: how did Locke end up this way? Did his unnatural connection to the island occur *after* he ran into the beautiful monster, or did it somehow exist even before that? We have to remember that John's miracles started occurring prior to his feet ever hitting the beach. Locke was wiggling his toes while the dying engines of Flight 815 were still roaring in the background... so what made him get up and walk?

Perhaps we get the answer to that question four and a half seasons later, as Jacob pays Locke a very important visit. Although he stops to see many of our main characters during *The Incident*, the few seconds Jacob spends with John may be the most critical. After being shoved out an eighth story window, Locke appears dead or at least unconscious by the time Jacob reaches him. But the second Jacob touches John's shoulder, he gasps for breath as if being brought back to life or even resurrected. In a very *Star Trek: Search for Spock* moment, it's very possible that Jacob *infused* Locke with something. Maybe even something that got reactivated later on, when he finally reached the shores of the island. Locke explains this to Boone later on, telling him: "This island, it changed me. It made me whole."

The long and short of this theory could better be put this way: maybe there's a part of Jacob *residing* in John Locke. When his faith is at its strongest, it can act through him. But when Locke's faith falters, maybe it has trouble continuing to use him as vessel. A good example of this occurs during *Deus Ex Machina*, when Locke temporarily loses the use of his legs. He mentions the island "taking away" its gift, but perhaps that explanation only covers Locke's limited interpretation of what's really happening here. Maybe Locke's legs are really still broken; maybe they never healed at all. Yet as long as John Locke has faith in the island, Jacob - or the entity put there by Jacob - can use them to walk anyway.

Locke as the Dark Monster

Continuing along these lines, the light monster probably isn't the only entity to manifest itself within John Locke. After living out a short life as Jeremy Bentham, Locke's physical body returns to the island in a coffin. Here's where the dark monster, or perhaps even Jacob's opponent, seizes the opportunity to become John. Maybe it required Locke to be dead before assuming his form, the same way it did for Yemi and Alex. The John Locke we see reborn on the island after the crash landing of Ajira Airways Flight 316 is not really John, at times anyway. Having both dark and light sides within him would explain much about Claire's vision of Locke in *Raised by Another*. In that dream sequence John looks up at Claire with two different colored eyes: black and white. The two opposing colors could easily be representing control from two different sources.

Post-Ajira, John's voice is also different at times. During a scene in *Dead is Dead,* Ben is rifling through his old desk at the Hydra office looking for a photo of him and Alex. When he finds it, Locke calls to him from out of frame: "What's that?" Listen to the voice here. It's way different from John Locke's voice; much deeper and sounding almost detached, as if the island itself were speaking through him. Later on in the same episode, a very frustrated Ben tells Locke "You don't have the first idea what the island wants." As Locke's eyes light up with an unnatural-looking fire he smirks, responding with: "Are you *sure about that*?" This time the voice change is even more pronounced - it's most definitely not Locke's voice. Something very cool and spooky is speaking through him, and Ben looks very fearful when he hears it.

And let's also not forget the scene in *Dead is Dead* where Benjamin Linus tries to summon the dark smoke monster to cast judgement on him. As the trees begin to rustle, Ben (and almost nine million viewers) look on anxiously... but instead of getting the monster we get none other than John Locke himself, striding almost comically out of the jungle once again. Shaken, Ben explains to Locke that he doesn't actually know where the monster is. Locke's immediate response: "I do."

After walking with him for the entire length of his journey, Locke also conveniently abandons Ben right before the smoke monster appears to him. You could chalk this up as Ben having to face judgement alone, or you could say that Locke and the monster can't both be in the same place at the same time for more obvious reasons. In any event, the cool thing to realize is that Locke was judging Ben's actions all along. All throughout this episode Locke's been pressing Ben to explain things he already has the answer to. He makes Ben admit and apologize for all types of actions, from strangling him to leading his people astray. More importantly however, Locke makes Ben understand that he himself is solely responsible for the death of Alex. Before stepping into the monster's chamber, Ben turns and admits this to Locke. "You were right", he tells him. "Why I needed to be judged... You were right. John, I did kill Alex. And now I have to answer for that. I appreciate you showing me the way, but I think I can take it from here."

Once Ben admits this, he's *already* been judged. The monster scene with the swirling flashbacks was just a formality. Locke, as the monster, has been judging Ben all along.

The Nail in the Coffin

If you're still not convinced that Locke's rocking a piece of the beautiful monster, pop in *Tabula Rasa* and fast-forward to the end. Watch the happy musical beach sequence in which Boone fixes Shannon's sunglasses, Sayid tosses Sawyer a mango, and Walt is reunited with his dog. Watch as the chirpy music fades to spooky silence - the camera zooming in on a *seriously* contemplative John Locke - and then jack up the volume and listen for the 'click-click-click' of the monster just before the LOST logo hits you in the face. (Thanks again to Karen, for showing me that one)

Hurley is the Indestructible Key to Everything

"I'm not supposed to be here."
- Hugo Reyes, *Left Behind*

"I'm sorry Hugo - You don't get to quit!"
- John Locke, *Everybody Hates Hugo*

"You make your own luck, Mr. Reyes. Don't blame it on the damn numbers."
- Martha Simms, *Numbers*

"Well, what if you weren't cursed? What if you were blessed?"
- Jacob to Hurley, *The Incident*

Back at the end of season three, I called Hurley "the indestructible epicenter of all things." *Through The Looking Glass* had just aired, and Hugo saved the day with nothing more than a Dharma van. I had a theory back then - one that still holds up pretty well - that Hurley's existence on the island was actually the key to the entire show. There's a lot of evidence that Hugo is special in some very unique ways, and he just might be the fly in the island's ointment.

As season five unfolded and we learned more about fate and free will, it seemed more and more like Hugo Reyes would turn out to be monumentally important. If Desmond is a constant, Hurley just might be a variable. It doesn't look like Hugo was ever supposed to be on the island at all - maybe even *both* times he arrived. That, coupled with his nagging desire to change things, might just make him a critical part of LOST's ultimate resolution.

Starting from the beginning, Hurley was the one person who shouldn't have been on the plane. He almost doesn't make flight 815, going through a pretty crazy series of random events to make it to the gate on time. First, his alarm clock doesn't go off because the outlet it was plugged into burned out. The elevator's full, forcing him to take the stairs. Driving to the airport, his car breaks down. Hugo has to run all the way through the airport in order to reach the ticket counter, and even then he arrives at the wrong terminal.

At the counter, the ticket agent delays him further. She even flat out tells him "I don't think you're supposed to be on this flight, dear." Hurley hijacks a scooter to get to the boarding gate, only to find that the jetway is closed. It truly does seem as if unknown forces are aligning against Hugo, trying to prevent him from getting on Oceanic 815. Only the gate agent Jenna actually helps Hugo to make his flight, and she very suspiciously turns out to be the same woman Desmond runs into years later as an archivist at the Oxford library.

Once Hurley arrives on the island we're given a glimpse into his charmed life. Hugo is somehow untouchable - both on the island and off. He seems surrounded by death and misfortune; collapsing decks, fires, lightning, a meteor strike, and now even a plane crash (or two). Although Hurley takes this to mean that he's cursed, he doesn't consider the possibility that none of these disasters are acts of God. It's more likely that they were acts of the island itself, desperately trying to correct one of its biggest problems: Hugo was never supposed to be there.

He even repeats this exact phrase in *Left Behind*. Standing pointedly alone and looking out over the ocean, Hurley exclaims "I'm not supposed to be here." In this scene he's actually talking to Sawyer (who is behind him), during an episode in which he cons his friend into being nice to everyone. But that's how LOST often works: through misdirection. Sometimes the answers are laid out right in front of us, but because we're concentrating on something else we don't always see them.

Another example of Hurley's disassociation to the island occurs during *Further Instructions*. As Boone is wheeling Locke through his vision of Sydney Airport, every one of the main characters is boarding Flight 815 except for two: Benjamin Linus (who was never on the plane to begin with), and Hurley. Instead of standing in line to board the plane like the rest of the passengers, Hugo is working the ticket counter. And in warning John about the upcoming danger all the rest of the characters would face, Boone's words to Locke are simple: "*Not* Hurley."

Hugo has always been lucky: rolling the dice, rocking at horseshoes, never missing at basketball, winning the lottery. As Leonard's wife tells him, Hurley makes his own luck. If this is the case, it stands to reason that he can also create his own future. Hugo makes his own kind of music - he's been doing this both on and off the island. He's untouchable, unreachable, and the island can't affect him for a very simple reason: he was never supposed to be there in the first place.

We see this early and often, too. In *Numbers,* Hurley escapes a trap and crosses a rope bridge that later collapses under Charlie's weight. He had a feeling he'd be alright, and he was. At the end of season three Hurley *knew* he could get that 30+ year old Dharma van to start... and sure enough the engine turns over. He drives the van into Pryce through a hail of gunfire, without ever taking a single bullet. In fact, Hugo's never been shot or wounded - a pretty big feat considering the track record of the rest of his friends. He gets captured by The Others along with Jack, Kate, and Sawyer, but for some reason Hurley was the one person they immediately let go.

If you buy into the theory that Hugo isn't supposed to be on the island to begin with, perhaps that's why it's unable to touch him. Because of this, maybe it's tried numerous ways to distract Hurley instead. It bribes him with a stash of food, but

Hugo dumps it. The second he does, more shows up (the food drop). It distracts him with romance in the form of Libby, up until she gets killed off. And since it can't reach him directly, the island even tries to get Hurley to commit suicide by showing up as Dave. Here it comes very close to convincing Hugo to jump off a cliff, but once again the plan doesn't work.

And in talking about what happens in *Dave*, we also have to consider Dave's take on what's really going on. He explains to Hurley that nothing on the island is real. Dave tells his friend that everything exists only in Hurley's head: "Every rock, every tree. Every tree frog. Even me. I'm part of your subconscious, man. All the people on this island are." Whether this is true or just the island trying to trick Hurley into killing himself, there's actually one really weird scene that backs up the theory that everything revolves around Hugo. Check out the ending of *In Translation*. There's another musical montage, but this one is stranger than most. Instead of fading out it abruptly stops at exactly the same moment that Hugo's walkman batteries die. It's as if the montage was only being played in Hurley's mind, and it ended when his batteries did.

The inability to control Hurley is even reflected outside in the real world. Hugo ends up back in Santa Rosa mental institution, where someone is watching over him to make sure he stays put. He gets out anyway, and is subsequently captured and imprisoned by the police. Somehow he escapes that situation too. No matter what happens, Hurley just can't be contained. He can't be touched. Hugo can somehow even see Jacob's cabin, because he's not affected by whatever illusions or smokescreens the island puts up to mask it. Because he's not bound by the rules, he might also be one of the few characters unable to "opt out" of the game. As Locke tells him during *Everybody Hates Hugo*: "I'm sorry Hugo. You don't *get* to quit."

Even examining some of the most innocuous dialogue, the writers flat out *tell us* that Hurley's not playing the same game as everyone else. During his stay in Santa Rosa, some of the mental patients are playing a game of basketball. As his friend Dave calls for the ball, one of the players passes it over his head and straight to Hurley, who's standing out on the sidelines. "Fantastic", Dave exclaims, "Give it to the guy who's NOT EVEN IN THE GAME!" A similar reference is made during *Lockdown*, where Hurley explains to Jack: "Maybe if I were in the loop I could be more helpful."

Toward the end of season five, it's no coincidence that Hurley is the one voice favoring the argument that things can be changed. He debates with Miles in Whatever Happened, Happened, and he tries to rewrite history with his *Empire Strikes Back* script. Hurley's seen more ghosts than anyone else, receiving their help and influence. Charlie comes to Hurley after dying, telling him "They need you." Who needs him? Everyone else in the story. The "Hurley bird" is even shrieking his name during two different season finales. It's possible that the answer's been right in front of us since the very beginning: Hurley could be the one person who'll end up changing things for good at the end of LOST.

Some final evidence for this theory exists at the end of season five. During *The Incident*, Jacob visits Hurley attempting to change the way he looks at things. Jacob suggests "What if you *weren't* cursed? What if you were blessed?" These words are actually enough to convince Hurley to board Ajira Airways Flight 316, taking him back to the island once again. Ben's surprise at seeing Hurley on the plane is evident in his first words to him: "Hugo, who told *you* to come?" This time the one person who shouldn't have made the original Flight 815 is included alongside the one person who was *supposed* to have been on board: Frank Lapidus. And to add even more fuel to Dave's assertion that everything is taking place in Hurley's head, he pulls a sleep mask down over his face for the trip back to the island.

The cool part of this theory is that most viewers of LOST have always figured the game changer would come from one of the bigger players: Jack, Locke, Ben, maybe even Desmond. Yet if you think about LOST in general, it makes sense that such changes would come from someone you'd least expect. Hurley is the perfect choice because no one's expecting him to matter. He's done nothing but cook, hand out food, play ping pong, and make everyone else laugh - including us.

Hugo Reyes is the island's very big problem because he's the one person who's *not* "here for a reason." As he himself says during *Numbers*, "I'm along for the ride." This alone might be the very reason why he'll end up being so important. The normal rules don't apply to Hurley, because he was never a part of the plan (timeline?) in the first place. If Faraday's assumption that "people are the variables" is true, Hugo Reyes could end up being the biggest variable yet. And if Hurley really is the ace up Jacob's sleeve, it could be why he was wearing an ace of spades T-shirt at his birthday party in *There's No Place Like Home*.

There is No Reality - Everyone is Sleeping

"It was only as real as you made it."
- Locke to Boone, *Hearts & Minds*

"Dude, this is all in your head."
- Hurley, *Exodus, Part 2*

"It's hard, I know, but I mean - all this? You, me, this island, that peanut butter... none of it's real, man. None of it's happening. It's all in your head, my friend."
- Dave to Hugo, *Dave*

"Nothing. We do nothing. It's not real. None of it's real."
- Jack, *Orientation*

It's a theory disdained by most of LOST's viewing audience, and one that's been categorically denied by the producers and writers of the show. Still, the sheer amount of evidence in favor of this theory requires that it be explored anyway: the idea that maybe nothing we've seen so far is real, and all of the main characters are actually dreaming.

Executive producer Carlton Cuse shoots down the dream theory with the following statement from the season two LOST DVD set: "What we have said and will continue to say is that we will not end the show with a cheat. It will not all have taken place in a snow globe, it will not all have been a dream." His words reflect the thoughts of most viewers: explaining LOST away as nothing but the dream of one or more characters is going to make us all feel pretty robbed for the last six years. No one wants to spend over half a decade getting emotionally attached to a bunch of characters that simply don't exist, or who exist only within someone else's mind.

With that said, there are many different angles and paths such a theory could take. Aside from the show being explained as someone's dream, it also could go any number of steps further in other, less literal directions. Taking *The Matrix* as one example, the final scene of LOST could pan out to reveal all of our main characters lying prone, head-to-head in a circle - maybe even an octagon - their minds wired together as some sort of big dreamlike experiment similar to the movie *The Cell*. Each character would be running through his or her own perceived version of the island's events, with people on the outside controlling what they see and encounter. Imagine Jack waking up, pulling wires away from his skull, peering through a darkened room to see himself surrounded by those who've already "left" the simulation: Boone, Shannon, Michael, Mr.

Eko, Charlie... Picture Jacob on one side of the room, his nemesis on the other, "playing" the game. Now imagine the sound of a ten million television screens being shattered across the world, all at once.

This is just one semi-funny example of how the producers could squeeze past their own denials. Do I think LOST will end this way? Probably not. But there's a hell of a lot of solid evidence that points to the fact that our characters are dreaming, sleeping, and most importantly, seeing the truth of things when they are closest to unconsciousness. And no matter how you slice it, that *means* something.

Transitional Unconsciousness

The show itself begins with Jack waking up, and this certainly isn't unintentional. Zooming in on his opening eye was a great camera trick, panning back to reveal the bamboo jungle we would spend most of LOST exploring. Jack is stunned and disorientated for a few moments, but that's to be expected considering he just crashed on the island. Sort of.

The fact is, we never actually see Flight 815 hit the beach. Everyone just sort of "wakes up" on the island. This motif is carried on in Locke's recollection of the crash during *Walkabout* - his eye opens, and he immediately hears the chaotic screams of fellow passengers. It's reflected even more strangely during *316*, when Jack wakes up in what looks to be the exact same position and circumstances of the first plane crash. Only this time around, we know Jack didn't crash on the island at all. He, Hurley, Kate, and Sayid were somehow zapped off their Ajira Airways flight, teleported to the island's surface, and brought back about 30 years in time to 1977. Kate puts it best: "What happened?"

If we can accept these circumstances during the Ajira 316 flight, who's to say the same thing didn't occur during the crash of Flight 815? Did *everyone* just wake up on the island the way Jack and Locke did? During the Pilot episode, Jack even tells Kate "I blacked out during the crash." It's interesting to note that in all of their midair flashbacks, the oxygen masks come down and our main characters put them right on. Jack and Rose do it quickly, and so does Charlie. Kate takes a long time with hers however, because she's helping the unconscious marshal with his mask first. If all the characters do wake up on the beach, then something had to make them go to sleep in the first place. Did the masks contain something to put the characters under? That idea is a pretty big stretch, but if so, perhaps this is why Kate tells Jack "I remember everything." She lasts longer than most because she put her mask on last, staying conscious long enough to even see the tail section get torn away.

But the placement of our characters on the island during *316* tells us a lot more than the original plane crash ever did. This was obviously the island's way of taking the characters it wanted, and putting them wherever (and whenever) it needed them to be. But is there more to it than that? Once again, everyone suddenly "wakes up" and doesn't remember how they got there. They recall the events leading up to their arrival on the island, but not the arrival itself.

The destruction of the Swan hatch is another great example of this. One minute our characters are one place... and then suddenly they wake up in another. They even make a point to show us that the hatch *imploded* rather than exploded. Where an explosion might have violently thrown these characters into the jungle, Locke, Eko, and especially Desmond were all deep inside - they should've been crushed and buried. Instead, they wake up elsewhere.

In *Further Instructions*, Locke actually comes to in a scene once again identical to Jack opening his eye in the Pilot episode, only this time with Desmond running naked through the jungle instead of Vincent. Later on during *Flashes Before Your Eyes*, we see Desmond wake up in not only the exact same way, but in *exactly the same spot*. Comparing those two eye-opening scenes, the view of the trees that both Desmond and Locke are given when they wake up is completely and totally identical in every way - branches, tree trunks and all.

This is a *huge* clue. Not only are these characters alive and well, they're both being "reset" to precisely the same starting point, much the way Jack was during *316*. They wake up in an impossible place, without any recollection of how they got there. And although we never see where Mr. Eko ended up after the Swan imploded, the fact that he was dragged off by a polar bear means we can't rule out the same scenario.

So why is waking up such an important part of LOST? Does the island put people under whenever it needs to move or arrange them? If so, it makes sense as far as maintaining each character's own personal level of believability. If something incredibly wild happens during the transition that would reveal what's really behind the curtain, then the island obviously can't show it to them. Making sure people are unconscious before moving them seems like a pretty logical choice.

This also explains the special orange juice cocktail everyone has to drink for the submarine ride to the island. Sawyer confirms this during *Namaste* when Jack asks about the incoming sub, telling him "Everyone gets knocked out before the trip." In *One of Us*, Richard whips up a tranquilizer cocktail for Juliet. "You're gonna want to be asleep for the trip Doctor Burke", he tells her. Ethan even laughs at that point, adding "It can be... kind of intense."

There are lots of other examples of transitional unconsciousness, with characters being knocked before being moved from one place to another. Jack, Sawyer, and Kate are all drugged for their trip to Hydra island in early season three, each of them waking up not sure how they got there. Some dozen episodes later, The Others put on masks and throw gas canisters, putting the main characters to sleep before moving out. Even in season one, when Danielle drugs Sayid, she apologizes to him as he wakes up. "Sorry about the sedative", she tells him. "It was the only safe way for me to *move* you."

Sleeping, Dreaming, and Waking Up

Characters are knocked out constantly on LOST. They're drugged, chloroformed, gassed, injected, pistol-whipped, rifle-butted, and shot with darts. If you watch LOST with this in mind, you'll see that there's someone sleeping or unconscious in just about every single episode. Sometimes they're dozing, but other times they're being put down intentionally by someone else. Locke drugs Boone in *Hearts & Minds*. Claire gets drugged by Ethan, and later knocked out by Danielle. Jack gets put under by Kate in *The Greater Good*, and also by Juliet (with Bernard's help) in *Something Nice Back Home*. Michael knocks Locke out, Locke knocks Sayid out, Sun knocks Ben out, and Charlie brains Desmond before diving down to the Looking Glass. The carnage goes on and on, with way too many references to keep listing here.

More importantly though, there appears to be a very powerful and direct relationship between unconsciousness and enlightenment. All throughout the show it seems that the closer a character gets to being put under, the more "in tuned" with the island he or she becomes. The state of unconsciousness or being asleep often results in strange dreams and visions, not to mention flashbacks and flash-forwards. In this way, the island actually tries to convey messages to LOST's characters while they're sleeping.

There are examples of this during every season. In *Raised by Another*, Claire's spooky vision of Locke warns her of the consequences of giving up Aaron. Charlie has multiple strange dreams, also about Aaron, during *Fire & Water*. And when Hurley falls asleep during *Everyone Hates Hugo*, the island communicates to him through an English-speaking version of Jin, telling him that "Everything is going to change."

In the case of Locke and Mr. Eko, the island even shows them events they can't possibly know about. In *Deus Ex Machina*, Locke witnesses the crash of the Nigerian Beechcraft that happened several years earlier, as well as a vision of Boone talking about his dead babysitter, Theresa. In the episode entitled *?*, Mr. Eko is granted a vision of Ana Lucia with blood streaming from her stomach and mouth. She even flat out tells him that he's dreaming, yet Eko would have no way of knowing at this point that Ana had been shot by Michael. He also dreams of his brother Yemi, who sits at the computer in the Swan hatch and foreshadows the results of the countdown clock reaching zero.

During *Cabin Fever*, Locke has another dream in which he sees Horace chopping down trees to build what would later become Jacob's cabin. Locke has never met Horace. He wouldn't know what he looked like, or that the blood running from his nose was a result of being killed by poison gas. What's strange about this vision is that the scene keeps repeating itself in a loop (indicating a residual "impression" of something that actually happened in the past), but Horace is still able to speak back and forth with Locke (indicative of intelligent interaction). Locke is seeing both the past and the present here, repeating itself over and over again, as the island delivers yet another message to help him ultimately find the cabin.

Yet in perhaps the most interesting of all these dreams, Locke actually *becomes* someone else. As Mr. Eko, he climbs the same cliff Boone did in season one. Upon reaching the top, a vision of Yemi sitting in Locke's wheelchair sharply tells him "Wake up, John!"

This isn't the first time one our characters are being told to wake up... not by a long shot. Even before Jack opens his eye in the very first scene of the show, another scene occurs between Christian Shephard and Walt's dog Vincent during LOST: Missing Pieces. In *So it Begins* (mobisode thirteen), Jack is still unconscious when Christian tells Vincent: "I need you to go find my son... I need you to *wake him up*... He has work to do."

Dreaming and sleeping are an integral part of LOST, with characters always trying to shake each other awake. The theme of coming around after being unconscious is even carried on within the flashbacks and flash-forwards. In *White Rabbit* we're given a parallel eye-opening scene, this time with a younger Jack waking up to a bully standing over him. In *Par Avion*, we see a younger version of Claire waking up after a bad car accident. Dave is trying to wake Hurley up from what he claims to be a coma. And in mobisode five, *Operation*

Sleeper, Juliet even tells Jack: "I've been living Benjamin Linus's dream for three years. Three years. It's time to wake up."

The Realm of Semiconsciousness

Jack would also be woken up by Juliet in *Something Nice Back Home*. As he suffers from appendicitis, Jack fades in and out of consciousness, with Juliet calling out to him. "Jack! Jack! Jack? I need you to wake up!" Listen carefully to this part, and you'll notice that at one point we actually hear *Kate's* voice in addition to Juliet's. Jack's perception is skewed by how close he is to falling back asleep, and this is not an accident. Because whatever our characters are seeing in their dreams, it's nothing compared to what they see when they're *close* to falling asleep, drugged, exhausted, delirious, or semiconscious.

Nowhere is this more evident than in *Further Instructions*. As Locke wakes up after the Swan implosion, he somehow knows he has to "speak to the island." The very first thing he does is build the sweat lodge - a rudimentary place very akin to the island's ancient, technology-shunning roots. Here Locke knows he'll be undisturbed, and he drugs himself with the same batch of trip-paste he used on Boone back in season one. This puts Locke into a meditative trance, where he gets one of the clearest and most purposeful visions we've seen on the entire show. By the time Boone is finished wheeling John through the Sydney airport, warning him and foreshadowing future events, Locke "wakes up" and knows exactly what needs to be done.

Locke played the same game in *Hearts & Minds*, only this time he drugged Boone to put him in touch with the island. "You need to let go", he tells his friend. Against his will, Boone then goes on to commune with the island through a vision in which his sister Shannon is killed by the monster. Instead of grief, Boone feels relieved. Locke then asks him "Is that what *it* made you see?" and when Boone questions whether his vision was real or not, Locke replies: "It was only as real as you made it." This is another allusion to the fact that reality, on the island at least, is a very relative term.

The lines of reality may get blurred by sleep, but they start disappearing altogether when a character is semiconscious or sleep-deprived. The first time Jack sees the image of his dead father, it's because by his own admission, he's not getting more than two hours of sleep a night. When he refuses to eat or drink after being captured by The Others, a very dehydrated Jack hears whispers (including his father's voice) over a long-broken intercom. Later on when he develops appendicitis, it's for another very specific reason: the island needs to commune with him. To do this, it needs him to sleep - and as we've seen throughout the show, Jack's not exactly one for sleep. Rose even questions how Jack could've gotten sick so suddenly during this same episode: "The day before we're all supposed to be rescued, the person that we count on the most suddenly comes down with a life-threatening condition, and you're chalking it up to bad luck?" When Bernard counters with "Well what are you saying, that... that Jack did something to offend the gods? People get sick, Rose", his wife replies simply: "Not here. Here, they get better."

Jack struggles valiantly to stay awake through his own operation, even after Juliet reveals that she's performed dozens of past appendectomies. There's no logical reason Jack needs to supervise her working on him at all. Yet somehow he wants to stay in control, almost as if Jack senses what the island is trying to do. "I don't want to be unconscious", he tells her. And when Juliet finally orders that Jack be put under, he fights to stay awake all the way until Bernard gives him a face full of chloroform. Jack then passes out and fades into a flash-forward... where he once again sees the walking dead image of his father, Christian.

Mr. Eko spends most of his last episode, *The Cost of Living*, fading in and out of consciousness from wounds he's received. As he does, Eko is granted images of the Nigerian warlords he killed, and even the altar boy Daniel who tells him to "confess." This could very well be the island showing him these things in an attempt to save Eko from the monster's upcoming judgement. Or perhaps these images are just other manifestations of the smoke monster itself, conjured up from Eko's memory when it scanned his mind in *The 23rd Psalm*.

An episode before that however, we see something even more interesting. Watch the scene during *Further Instructions* in which Locke and Charlie put Eko down to rest for a moment. As Charlie conveniently runs off to get water, Locke speaks to an unconscious Eko, apologizing to him and accepting responsibility for his friends being captured. At this point, Eko is still fully knocked out... but he speaks to Locke anyway. "You can still protect them. You can still save them", Eko says, looking blankly up at the sky.

This isn't Eko talking, here. The island is *speaking through him*. When Charlie comes back into the scene, Eko's eyes are closed again, as if he never spoke at all. Because he's close to delirium, the island can somehow access and use Eko. In a way, perhaps we're seeing a type of temporary possession. And as the island delivers these words to John, it even includes a personal message - one that pertains directly to his own thoughts and flashbacks this episode: "After all", it explains to him, "You are a *hunter*, John."

An even more dramatic example of the island speaking through someone occurs one season earlier during *What Kate Did*. As Sawyer is delirious from his infected bullet wound, Kate tends to him. As she's mashing up some fruit, Sawyer suddenly jerks awake and grabs Kate by the throat, shouting "Why did you kill me? Why did you kill me!" This time, it's actually Kate's father Wayne speaking to his daughter through Sawyer's semiconscious state. He's on her mind this episode, and what she did to him dominates her flashbacks. Eerily, Kate even recognizes what's happening here. Later in the episode she addresses Sawyer as Wayne, and then starts explaining why she took the steps she did. Once again this happens when no one else is around, lending to the theory that maybe each character is only perceiving these things in his or her own mind. Whatever the case, the island seems hellbent on getting them to admit to, feel guilty, or apologize for their past misdeeds.

So why does reaching a state of unconsciousness seem to bring someone closer to the island's "other side?" Delirium appears to create some type of direct connection between the underworld of the island and the life that our characters believe to be real. With sleeping, dreaming, or semiconscious characters acting as a conduit, messages are sent back and forth. But what's real and what's not real? And just which side of reality are our characters on?

Reality... In the Eye of the Beholder

While all this existential talk tends to scare many fans off, we really need to explore the directions the writers seem to be going with LOST. On the island we've seen monsters and ghosts, the walking dead, whispers from characters who are no longer around, and many, many references to things that simply don't exist in the "real world." Many people will use a blanket explanation here, saying "Well, the island is special", as if this suddenly accounts for everything strange we've seen so far. But when you're dealing with immortality, time travel, and subterranean wheels that move entire land masses? Even the most diehard realist has to wonder if something else is actually up.

There are various moments throughout LOST where reality is brought into question. Dave trying to coax Hurley out of his living dream is a prime example. In a scene straight out of *Total Recall*, Dave works on convincing Hugo that nothing he's experiencing is real. He tells him that in all actuality, Hugo is stuck in a coma "In your own private Idaho, inside Santa Rosa." Hurley even comes close to believing his imaginary friend, almost killing himself in the process.

Now take Kate's childhood friend Tom's words for a moment, in *Born to Run*. As Kate flashes back to the moments before his death, Tom tells her "If you cooperate, you can have a *real life*." As viewers, we've traditionally seen the off-island flashbacks as the "real world", and the on-island sequences as a fantastic version of some very twisted events. But imagine for a moment: what if both sides of the coin were an illusion? What if there was no real life until the characters reached enlightenment, at which point they'd be allowed to return to reality? Could the flashbacks be imaginary too? Or are the writers playing games with us when Kate walks past a sign in the hospital that reads "Magnetic Resonance *Imagining*?" The same thing goes for the "Use Your Imagination" poster we see in the Dharma schoolhouse, four seasons later.

The validity of certain events on the island becomes an issue also, especially the Swan's countdown timer. As the quintessential man of science, Jack tries telling Locke "It's not real. None of it's real." But as the man of faith, Locke somehow convinces Jack that pushing the button is real *and* important. Later on however, even Locke loses faith before the season is out. He assumes Jack's role of denial and Mr. Eko assumes John's old role of the faithful. At this point Locke is the one telling him "No, it's not real. We're only puppets... puppets on strings." He also goes on to say "As long as we push it, we'll never be free..." a nice little phrase that foreshadows the future battle between fate and free will, destiny and change.

Very often, it seems as if reality or answers lie just beyond the reach of our characters. There are many times when, just as they're about to discover something important, the moment gets snatched away. Take the somewhat out of place conversation that happens between Kate and Claire, in *White Rabbit*. Claire asks Kate if she's seen any hairbrushes. When Kate tells her no, Claire responds with "I must have looked through 20 suitcases and I can't find one. It's weird, right? You'd think that everyone packs a hairbrush..." Before Claire can finish making this observation however, she clutches her head and almost falls down. It's as if someone or something interrupted her before she could continue making her point. "You alright?" Kate asks her, to which Claire responds "Yeah, it's just the heat. Oh, and I'm pregnant."

Truth be told, it *is* strange that there aren't any hairbrushes on the island. Claire's point is a pretty good one. And just as all the characters have arrived on the island "for a reason", this dialogue must there for a reason too. It's not like the writers of LOST to waste a scene, which lends believability to the theory that maybe someone didn't want Claire continuing her little hairbrush investigation at that moment.

In *Par Avion*, Sayid questions the limits to Mikhail's knowledge of the 815 survivors. "Don't speak to us as if you know us", he tells him. But Mikhail answers him smugly: "Of course I don't know you, Sayid Jarrah. How could I? And you, Kate Austen, are a complete stranger to me. But you John Locke, you I might have a fleeting memory of, but I must be confused. Because the John Locke I know was paral-" At this exact moment, Danielle Rousseau interrupts Mikhail by discovering the sonic fence. "Hey! Look at this! Over here...come on" - her very words are those of a magician, one trying to distract the crowd from looking one way by directing their attention in another. Mikhail was just about to reveal something pretty big here: he knows that Locke was once paralyzed. But before this revelation could take place, something else happened to disrupt it.

This occurs again during *Not in Portland*. Jack's working on removing Ben's tumor as Tom Friendly looks on. As Jack begins asking why The Others didn't just take Ben off-island to have his operation, Tom tells him "Because ever since the sky turned purple-" Before Tom can finish his sentence, blood spurts up from Ben's spine, interrupting the rest of what he was about to say. Jack explains that he must've nicked an artery, but this time not on purpose. It's important to note that this scene occurs long after Jack makes a bid for his friends' freedom by putting an intentional incision in Ben's kidney sac. Did someone just push the "burst an artery" button? Because just as it seems a main character is about to make a revelation or discover something important, an incredibly convenient distraction occurs. Jack didn't do this - not even by accident. Something else stopped Tom from finishing his sentence, as if he were about to reveal too much.

It's entirely possible that there's a higher power - if not the island itself - watching over the characters on LOST, intervening whenever it deems necessary. If you explore the theory that nothing the characters are seeing is real, then *something* needs to guard the tenuous line between illusion and reality.   Characters who step over that line might suddenly realize where they are, and would then become dangerous to the rest of the cast. It could be compared to having a lucid dream: once you actually realize that you're dreaming, you might start telling everyone else within your dream that none of what they're seeing is real.

The line between what's real and unreal is often vague, but sometimes we see boundaries. In *Hunting Party*, Tom Friendly even draws a line in the sand, perhaps as a metaphor for this very idea. "Right here, there's a line", he tells the 815 survivors. "You cross that line, we go from misunderstanding to... something else." As if to further illustrate the point, in the same episode Jack's father Christian tells him: "Careful. There's a line, son. You know it's there. And pretending its not... that would be a mistake."

Identity... Also in the Eye of the Beholder

Of course the possibility exists that we're seeing real characters with real lives, thrust into a very extraordinary situation. But by the same token, if everything else on LOST is fake or contrived, we also have to question the validity - and even the identity - of the characters themselves. Deception has been a huge part of the show from the very beginning, ever since Kate found the fake beard and theatrical glue in the locker room of the Staff station. And as Walt refers to The Others during *Three Minutes*: "They're not who they say they are. They're pretending."

So is Walt making reference to The Others playing dress up for most of season two? Sure. But before you draw the line right there, let's start counting up all the other references to dual identity within LOST.

Benjamin Linus starts things off by pretending to be Henry Gale. "Whoever you think I am, I'm not" - these are his words to Sayid while being help captive in the Swan's armory. These same words would also be repeated by Juliet, spoken to Richard Alpert in *Not in Portland*. We'd hear them yet again, spoken to Mikhail by Sayid during *Enter 77*: "I'm not who you think I am." Sayid actually refutes his identity twice this episode, as he also denies being the man who tortured Amira in his flashback. Later on during *He's Our You*, he'd also tell

Ben "I'm not what you think I am."

Throughout every season, many aspects of LOST have been a big masquerade. Ana Lucia pretends to be a prisoner of the tail section survivors. Charlie pretends to be an Other when he abducts Sun. Both Goodwin and Ethan pretend to be people they're not: survivors of Flight 815. James Ford becomes Sawyer, Michael Dawson becomes Kevin Johnson, and Kate has almost as many aliases as Anthony Cooper. And for reasons we still don't know, Dr. Pierre Chang goes by two other names: Edgar Hallowax and Mark Wickmund. Throw in all the other instances of duplicate names, faces, and similar-looking characters we've seen throughout LOST, and reality beats a hasty retreat. Something is definitely up.

All of these pseudonyms barely scratch the surface when it comes to people pretending to be someone they're not. In some cases, even inanimate objects aren't what they appear to be. During *The Hunting Party*, Michael points to the Swan's computer and tells Jack: "That thing is not what you think it is. You don't understand, man. You don't have *any* idea." This occurs just after Mike somehow used it to "talk" to his son again. So does Walt have some pretty convenient computer privileges back at The Other's encampment? Is Michael buck-wild crazy? Or is reality something that exists on a person-to-person, perception type basis?

As our main characters begin to question the strange events of the island, they also question the people they run into. The largest recurring identity crisis occurs within a phrase we hear literally *dozens* of times throughout the show: "Who are you?" The characters of LOST have put this question to each other countless times, as well as to everyone else they've encountered along the way. There have also been critical moments where the answer to this question isn't so easy. In *The Cost of Living*, Eko demands "Who are you? Who are you!" while confronting the smoke monster, appearing before him as his brother Yemi. And in *The Incident*, Hurley asks Jacob perhaps the biggest question of all: "Who *are* you, dude?"

But to blur these lines even further, sometimes the characters question their *own* identities. In one of LOST's most oddly-placed episodes, *Stranger in a Strange Land*, Jack travels all the way to Thailand to find himself after difficulties with his father; at this point he's already on a journey of self-discovery. After following his lover Achara to discover where she secretly goes at night, Jack takes her for a tattoo artist. Achara clarifies her need for secrecy by explaining that she has a gift: "I am able to *see* who people are... and I mark them." In her own words, she actually "defines" them. Jack goes angrily out of character here. He asks, "Do you see who I am, Achara?" When she answers yes, Jack's eyes glaze over almost manically. He throws her up against the nearest wall and pins her there, demanding: "Who am I?" Jack then forces Achara to mark him, despite her warning that there will be consequences. This occurs during the same episode in which Juliet is physically marked, apparently as an excommunication from The Others.

This whole episode is strange, and not just because the word is used twice within the title. It's also not a fan favorite, rated one of the least-popular episodes amongst LOST fans. Within it however, I think we get some considerable clues. Jack's wild questioning of his true identity seems oddly important, and Juliet's own mark seems strange as well. For someone who was brought to the island in a submarine to do fertility research, painfully branding her in the back seems a pretty excessive way to boot her off. We have to wonder if Charles Widmore was marked the same way when he was exiled from the island, or if he's somehow still included in The Others' sacred group. Either way, Isabel presents an even deeper mystery when she translates the characters on Jack's tattoo: "He walks amongst us, but he is not one of us." Jack agrees with her translation, telling her "That's what they say", but then goes on to shake his head. "It's not what they mean."

So what exactly *do* the characters on Jack's tattoo mean? Obviously he walks amongst the survivors of Flight 815... are we supposed to believe he's really not one of them? Is Jack somehow different and separate, in the same way Locke seems to be? Personally, I think it's a pretty safe bet. Take this excerpt from the story Jack reads Aaron during *Something Nice Back Home*: "I wonder if I've been changed in the night. Let me think. Was I the same when I got up this morning? But if I'm not the same, the next question is, 'Who in the world am I?' Aha, that's the great puzzle." Being changed, sleeping, and questioning one's own identity are all common themes that are grounded deeply within the core of LOST, especially for Jack.

Back to the subject of John Locke, take Boone's own words regarding him: "Do you know who this guy *is*?" At times, it's almost as if certain characters are more than just the sum of their flashbacks. All of these questions related to identity could be taken as just a little bit more than repetitive coincidence. At one point, Locke even dreams that he's not himself. In the episode entitled *?*, he has a vision in which he appears as someone completely different: Mr. Eko. If the island was trying to show John that Eko needed to climb the cliff, why wouldn't Eko have been the one to receive the dream? Did we just see the island slip up? Is it possible that we saw something important here?

But the best evidence that something's going on with character identity is also the most chilling. To understand what I'm talking about, you'll need to put this book down for a minute and get out your LOST season two discs. Cue up episode fourteen, *One of Them*. Now jump to the scene in which Sayid is about to torture Benjamin Linus (as Henry Gale). Here, Sayid builds tension as he explains his origins as a torturer to his captive. And right before the infamous line in which he introduces himself by name, Sayid puts a strange and very unnerving question to Ben: "You want to know who I am?"

Listen to this line. It's definitely *not* Sayid who says it. The voice is sinister, otherworldly, and even mechanical. Once again the camera tricks us here, showing us the back of Sayid's head (and the front of Ben's terrified face) as the line is delivered. In the whole scene, it's one of the only lines where we don't get a frontal view of Sayid as he talks. This is because Sayid is not talking. Maybe physically, yes - but at this exact moment something else is speaking through him. And perhaps Ben knows it.

Character Roles

As if to help out with all the character struggles concerning who's who, we also see the Flight 815 survivors identifying themselves, and each other, as having specific roles. Sawyer leads this off in the Pilot episode, telling Jack "Whatever you say doc, you're the hero." Jack does a good job of playing out this role. He leads the crash survivors to food and water and lives up to his surname, Shephard, by herding them to the debatable safety of the caves. Jack also plays the role of doctor, right down to being the sacrificial physician who gives his own blood to the point of nearly passing out. His titles of hero and doctor carry over to the off-island world as well. After saving a pair of crash victims on the Sixth Street Bridge during *Through The Looking Glass*, one of his associates even calls him "Doctor Shephard, the hero. Twice over."

Early on, Sawyer actually identifies many roles. He tells his fellow survivors: "Fine. I'm the criminal. You're the terrorist

(Sayid). We can all play a part." Turning to Shannon, Sawyer asks "Who do you wanna be?" Her lack of a role is even called into question later on by Locke, who tells her: "Everyone gets a new life on this island, Shannon. Maybe it's time you start yours."

In *Homecoming*, Jack also assigns roles. While dividing up the guns, he says: "Alright, Sayid, you're the soldier. Locke, you're the hunter." In *White Rabbit*, Sawyer gives Kate the marshal's badge, telling her "You're the new sheriff in town." In *All The Best Cowboys Have Daddy Issues*, we find out that Locke and Kate also fulfill the role of tracker: "We've got two trails", Jack tells everyone, "And apparently, two trackers." And in *The Moth*, Charlie gets assigned a very unique role by Liam: "You're the rock god, baby brother!"

It's almost like fleshing out characters in a book. Good and evil are also personified, with identities all their own. During season one, Charlie assigns a role to their biggest nemesis: "Ethan... Ethan's the bad guy." But by the end of season two, Ben disagrees. "We're the good guys", he tells Michael, leading to a very "us vs. them" mentality. This is perpetuated even further through the episode titles *One of Them* and *One of Us*, creating a rivalry that would stretch deep into the show's plotline until more dangerous enemies would emerge.

Each of these roles serves not only to give each character an identity, but also a purpose. As strangers waking up on a strange island, they fall effortlessly into the roles that are dictated by their flashbacks. Jack continues being a doctor.

Michael continues being an engineer. Sayid even continues being a torturer, although you wouldn't think such a job would be needed amongst a bunch of crash survivors. It seems almost a little bit too convenient, and at times, somewhat contrived. And if you're considering a theory that actually questions reality, you have to once again question the flashbacks and flash-forwards we're being shown. In fact, just who is showing us these things? Are they legitimate, accurate representations of our main characters' past experiences? Or instead, are the flashbacks *themselves* being tailored to fit each individual person's assigned role on the island?

Role Reversals

Accepting roles the characters are assigned at the beginning of the show is all well and good... but watching them repeatedly swap roles like they're changing clothing is a whole different ball game. Throughout five seasons we've seen LOST move backward, forward, and sometimes even sideways. We've witnessed an awful lot of character development, and this is to be expected. But what's not expected are the sudden role reversals and occasional reassignments that get scattered from season to season, episode to episode. At times they seem to happen almost instantly: good becomes bad, captors become captives, and to draw yet another mirror-image analogy, things often end up backward in the blink of an eye.

"Wait? Now you're a tracker?" Boone's words to Kate in season one foreshadow a lot more role reversals later on down the road. Locke also warns Jack off his own role, telling him: "Go back, be the doctor. Let me be the hunter." Locke makes an outstanding Hunter for several seasons, but eventually takes on the role of leader when Ben hands him the gauntlet in *The Other Woman*. He tells John: "Well, you're the leader now. I know it's a tough position."

Some of the more dramatic changes occur within the most important characters. Jack goes from being a leader to a follower over the course of the show. By *Namaste*, he's relegated to Dharma janitorial work. Moreover, Jack seems totally content with this turn of events. Having once been a devout man of science, Jack is now a man of faith, completely happy to roll with whatever fate the island has in store for him next. Sawyer also undergoes a very radical change. Once a loner, con-man, and convict, he suddenly finds himself in the mid 1970's as head of Dharma security. Where he used to be responsible for only himself, he's now taken on the responsibility of caring for and protecting more than a hundred people. Eko and Locke also swap positions over the course of season two, trading off the faith and science roles that wind up causing the destruction of the Swan hatch.

Situational roles are traded off as well. Jack goes from captor to captive. Sayid goes from torturer to the one being tortured. Kate goes from eternal fugitive to happy homemaker, even though that role doesn't quite work out for her. And

Juliet of course, makes the difficult transition from *One of Them* to *One of Us*.

As our main characters board Ajira Flight 316, we see even more definitive versions of role reversals when compared to the original Flight 815. Sayid is now Kate - shackled, sullen, and accompanied by his own law-enforcement official, Illana; the male/female roles are even reversed here as well. Kate is now Claire - broken, confused, and torn over a decision she just made regarding her child. Ben arrives to board the plane much the same way Hurley did in season one, having just made the flight at the very last second. Hurley even flat out tells him "You're not supposed to be here." And as for Hugo himself, it looks like he stays exactly the same... as always. Only this time instead of plugging headphones into his ears, Hurley covers his eyes with a sleep mask for the ride back.

See You on The Other Side...

The idea that our characters might be experiencing some sort of blurred reality is nothing new. With references to imagination, hallucination, dreams, ghosts, and visions... most viewers can agree that there's probably something fishy going on. Although the island has some fantastic supernatural elements to it, there's also something happening *behind* the scenes that we're not quite aware of just yet. Sometimes it feels like we get a glimpse of it though. It's almost like seeing something in your peripheral vision, and then turning your head to find out nothing's there. The characters experience this too, and it seems to be happening more and more as we reach the end of the show.

Ben's "whatever you imagined, whatever you wanted to be" speech to Locke back in season three is not something that's going to be explained away very easily. As LOST draws to a close, it probably shouldn't surprise us to find that certain aspects of the show may have been nothing more than fabrication. Whether these illusions are created by the characters themselves or by a higher level of authority doesn't matter so much. What does matter is what's real and what's not real, and at exactly what point the curtain was pulled down over our eyes.

So is LOST nothing but a big dream? Are the characters really asleep in their seats on Flight 815, and is the "whoosh!" sound we hear before every flashback just the roar of the plane's engines outside? Not if the ABC Studio doesn't want a full-blown riot on their hands. But for the writers and producers of the show, it sure seems like they're having fun playing around with the concept. Especially the person who put the words "Dream Machine" across the top of Hurley's alarm clock in season one.

Multiple Realities and Alternate Timelines

"We're not supposed to know each other."
- Juliet, *Namaste*

"I'm sorry Pen...we're not supposed to be together."
- Desmond, *Flashes Before Your Eyes*

"You're not supposed to go home."
- Locke, *There's No Place Like Home*

"Well, I got some bad news for you, Jack. You don't belong here at all."
- Daniel Faraday, *The Variable*

Getting closer to the end of LOST means getting more and more answers. Lately, that's involved some pretty radical ideas regarding what happened to the survivors of Flight 815... and what theoretically *should have* happened to them. For a while, the paradoxes of time travel were discussed only in the show's chat rooms and message boards. But now? These theories are being brought up by the characters themselves, including hint-laden dialogue that has our heads spinning with the many fantastic possibilities for season six.

In *The Variable*, Daniel Faraday speaks to Jack and Kate about changing destiny. He plans on using Jughead to prevent the Swan hatch from being built, which in turn would prevent Flight 815 from ever crashing. He tells them: "Your plane will land, just like it's supposed to, in Los Angeles." After watching the reverse-colored LOST logo during the season five finale, it looks like something may have actually changed. There's a pretty good chance we'll see this at the beginning of season six, with Oceanic Flight 815 making it safely to LAX - all passengers and crew alive and accounted for. If and when this happens, most people will view the events that follow as an alternate reality or timeline to the one we've been watching since the show aired.

But the interesting part of Dan's last sentence are the words "supposed to." What Faraday is trying to say here is that Flight 815 was *always destined* to land safely. That makes everything we've seen on the show the alternate reality: all five seasons of LOST, right up until the detonation of Jughead's core. It also makes everything we see after Flight 815 lands - if it lands at all - the *true* reality or timeline. And for those of us who've seen *Donnie Darko*, we all know what that means.

Assuming Oceanic 815 was supposed to arrive at LAX, Desmond's lack of action in the Swan hatch caused a different, alternate set of circumstances to occur. From here, the universe spun off an alternate timeline or reality in which the plane actually crashed on the island. But at the same time, the plane *should've* landed - or perhaps even did land - in Los Angeles. If we're to accept Faraday's assertion that this is what was supposed to really happen, then the plane, the people, and the crazy set of events we've seen on the island are nothing more than one big messy anomaly that needs to be corrected.

Getting back to reality (or unreality), this would mean we've been watching an alternate timeline for the last five years. The main characters aren't dreaming at all... they're real people in a real situation. They are however, stuck in a parallel universe where they don't belong. In short, they're LOST. And because they're all misplaced, maybe they're not totally bound by the same laws and rules of their original timeline. Getting back to the "real" world has always been their goal, whether they knew it or not.

This would make everything we've seen a part of this alternate timeline, including the off-island world that the Oceanic Six briefly visited. But it would also explain why it seemed so desperately critical that they never leave the island at all; in that world, these six lives are already accounted for. Flight 815 crashed into the Sunda Trench, killing everyone on board. None of the characters who escaped the island would have a place in that universe, which may be why they can't kill themselves. Michael unsuccessfully tries suicide numerous times in *Meet Kevin Johnson*, and Jack gets conveniently distracted before he can throw himself off a bridge in *Through The Looking Glass*. If the plane on the bottom of the Indian Ocean really is Oceanic 815, then these characters are dead already. Hurley even tells this to Jack during *Something Nice Back Home*: "Cause we're dead... all of us. We never got off that island."

Paradoxical Issues

Without getting too deep into the plotline of *Donnie Darko*, a similar situation happens. The paradox of someone (Donnie) showing up in a timeline where he didn't truly belong threatened to destroy the very fabric of the universe if it wasn't corrected in time. Dramatic, I know... but still a great movie. Time travel, airplanes, and duplicate objects existing in the same timeline (in this case, a jet engine) all take place as well. And when we compare this to LOST's plotline of getting the O6 back to the island quickly, Ms. Hawking seems similarly worried about the apocalyptic consequences of failure.

In *Donnie Darko* however, the situation that resulted in the paradox was purely accidental - an airplane was in the wrong place at the wrong time. On LOST, we now know our characters arrive on the island because they've been intentionally summoned there. During *The Incident*, we learn that this was probably through the will of Jacob. As Locke has already jammed down our throats, everyone on the island is "here for a reason", even though we have yet to see just what that reason is. Looking at it from a universal perspective however, the characters aren't really "supposed to be here" at all. This is a viewpoint shared by Jacob's nemesis as well, judging from his unfavorable reaction to seeing the Black Rock at the season finale fish-fry.

The alternate timeline theory has been around for a while now, and it's always met stiff viewer resistance. Recently however, it's gained a lot more acceptance - due largely to the fact that the writers and producers seem like they might be going down that road. Time travel was another big theory that was met with laughter and skepticism for quite some time... up until it actually happened. But with the show doing such a great and careful job of it in season five? Very few people are complaining anymore.

Executed sloppily, the introduction of alternate timelines could easily careen out of control, leaving a messy jumble of inexplicable events and impossible paradoxes in its wake. By the same token however, it could also explain some of the more obscure pieces of LOST's puzzle. In an alternate universe, anything can happen. Locke can walk again. Rose can be cancer-free. It can explain how Pierre Chang can be Mark Wickmund in the Pearl Orientation video, and can still have the use of the arm he injured during *The Incident*.

With the island defined as a place where multiple universes converge, it makes virtually anything possible. Perhaps it even acts as the ever-roaming nexus for all of these timelines, with the island's movements finally pinned down and mapped out by whoever built the Lamp Post. Slipping in and out of these mirrored universes, it's not a stretch to say the island can pick things up and drop things off - like polar bears into the Tunisian desert. This would easily explain why the island is so hard to find and even more difficult to reach. As Ben says in season two, "God can't see this place."

And while the island keeps moving perhaps things are constantly changing, like the stitched-up scar on Doc Ray's face as he floats through the time-storm and washes up on shore. Just as Hurley's radio picks up songs from the past, people already gone can come back as ghosts or visions: dead (as ghost Charlie nods in agreement with Hurley at Santa Rosa), but in some ways not really dead at all. You could even suggest that the characters from one universe might actually be *watching* themselves in another, their own hurried voices making up whispers that bleed through from one timeline to the next. In fact, we've already seen characters on LOST who have watched themselves. Locke - or at least the entity possessing Locke at the time - witnesses Richard treat his wound at the Beechcraft during *Follow The Leader.* And in a very strange scene during *Maternity Leave,* Claire is actually shown standing within her own flashback for a split second, as she watches herself interact with Ethan.

Cleaning up The Mess of the Past

We can't really explore the future of the alternate reality

theory without going out on a limb, and to be brutally honest, several limbs. If we assume that Faraday was correct about Jughead changing destiny, then let's pretend for a moment that Juliet succeeded in setting off the bomb. Oceanic Flight 815 lands at LAX. Everyone gets off the plane unharmed, even the characters who have previously died, with no recollection of the island at all. It's also September of 2004 again.

Would this undo the events of the last five seasons of LOST? Maybe, but maybe not. In the event of multiple universes, the timeline that got split off when Flight 815 hit the beach would still occur. There would essentially be two of everything, separated by some wacky curtain of simultaneous existence. The phrase "see you on the other side" takes on a whole different meaning once you realize that there really *is* another side, or as Desmond keeps putting it, "another life." The events on the island as we've seen them so far would still unfold, but at the same time, the people on board Oceanic 815 who landed in Los Angeles would be living out their own lives concurrently.

So now let's go out even further on a limb. What if the characters getting off the plane in LAX did maintain some memory of past events? Would that change anything for them, or would Jack, Kate, Sawyer and everyone else have one last big high-five before going on to live separate lives again? In such a case, you have to wonder what the consequences would be of being split existentially down the middle. Would our characters have dreams or nightmares? Would the island still chase after them? Would Ms. Hawking come knocking on Jack's door in the middle of the night, claiming that the world's going to end again?

In all likelihood, probably. Because for whatever reason, Jacob brought these people to the island to accomplish something, and he's not going to let them go that easily. He needs to finish the game - to prove to his adversary that there really is an ending. By bringing the survivors of Flight 815 to the island, he's enlisting their help. The only problem with the scenario so far is that it ends in a nuclear blast... or at least, it does by the end of season five.

So now let's take the universe in which everyone from Flight 815 lands safely in Los Angeles. If the island, its agents, The Others, or even Illana and Bram's people can somehow enlist their aid, perhaps they could reach back through to the other side and help *themselves* accomplish the correct goals. Remember that if this happens, it's September 23rd of 2004 again. The day they land in LAX is the same day everyone wakes up amongst the flaming wreckage of the Pilot episode in the alternate timeline. If the characters who have already been through the island's events can somehow reach or influence the ones just starting off after the plane crash, perhaps they can actually generate a different outcome.

Maybe the "ghost" of Charlie that Hurley sees at Santa Rosa hospital during *The Beginning of The End* is really a projection of the Charlie who lands safely in LA, come to warn him that he needs to return to the island. Ditto for the ghost of Ana

Lucia who pulls Hugo over to offer him advice during *The Lie*. And just as Ms. Hawking showed us that the Lamp Post station could be used to track the island's position, perhaps there's also some way to communicate with the people who are stuck there. If so, the whispers our characters have been hearing in the jungle for the last five seasons could very well be *their own voices*. Created by alternate versions of themselves, these whispers would be watching and waiting... monitoring the on-island events like a bunch of spectators until the moment comes when the 815 crash survivors are about to make a choice they're not supposed to (calling the freighter?), so they can somehow step in and prevent that event from happening.

Admittedly, that's an awful lot of "what ifs" and "maybes" strung out in a row. But if things played out this way, it would reveal who the 3rd player in LOST's big game really is: the characters themselves. As Faraday says to Jack: "Us. We're the variables!" And to flow right alongside another common theme of the show, the characters would essentially be cleaning up their own mess. This hint was dropped in the middle of the brainwashing video in Room 23: "We are the causes of our own suffering."

Since they've lived through it all before, the characters have an idea of what they're supposed to do... and not supposed to do. At critical times, they could even reveal themselves to their on-island counterparts, such as Walt showing up to help a gut-shot Locke as he lay bleeding in the Dharma pit of death. Hell, this could even explain the reversed voices we hear at times: our characters projecting backward to prior events in the island's timeline. Far fetched? Sure. But when you're trying to predict season six based upon seasons one through five, sometimes you've got to skate on some pretty thin ice.

Finally, we should also consider what happens if Flight 815 lands at LAX in an entirely different universe than the one it took off from. As everyone gets off the plane, maybe they'll find out that a good many things have changed. Story-wise, we have a whole season left to go. Something sure needs to drive our characters to keep caring about the on-island events, or they'd each fade back into their own unhappy off-island lives. And not only would that be boring, but it would undo all of the great character transformations we've seen over the last five seasons.

Questioning Our Existing Timelines

When it comes to alternative realities, perhaps there's even evidence that things have changed already. As Frank Lapidus pilots Ajira 316 to a crash landing in 2007, we hear the original Dharma tower transmission playing on the co-pilot's radio as he attempts his Mayday call. This would be impossible - time-wise, anyway - because Rousseau had already changed the message to her own voice in the late 1980's. On top of this, we also watched her turn the radio tower's message completely off two seasons prior to Flight 316's arrival.

The radio tower continues to be the source for inexplicable

mystery during *This Place is Death*. Way back in 1988, the French science team also picks up the strange looped transmission. Only this time, many fans of LOST listening to the recording can actually hear Hurley's own voice within it, repeating some of the numbers. If this is somehow the case, it means that Hurley *is* responsible for his own suffering, as he becomes the very person who gave Leonard Simms the numbers in the first place. It seems an impossibility from what we've seen so far, because we never watched Hurley go anywhere near the radio tower while stuck in 70's Dharma... unless a universe somehow exists where this actually happened.

The plot device of alternate timelines is definitely pretty far out there. Unlike the other theories in this book, the ideas involving our characters living out their lives within parallel universes are very sketchy, with little to no evidence to back them up. The whole concept also seems a much too scientific way of explaining away some of the more magical moments we've experienced on the island (for more information on this topic, see *Midi-chlorians*). At this point, such an interpretation is almost too cold and clinical for LOST, but we'll just have to see where the story goes.

The Oceanic Six Storyline Never Really Happened

"Sorry, but we have to lie."
- Sayid, *The Lie*

"I know why you don't want to see the baby, Jack. But until you do...until you want to, there's no you and me going for coffee."
- Kate, *Eggtown*

"All the Oceanic Six... we're all dead. We never got off that island."
- Hurley, *Something Nice Back Home*

"Who's... Aaron?"
- Carole Littleton, *The Little Prince*

One theory I put forth last season didn't sit well with most people, and that was the idea that the entire O6 storyline never happened. For some reason people have little trouble believing in smoke monsters and time travel... but suggest for one moment that someone's experiences are fabricated or false, and suddenly you've got some very fierce opposition. There are many viewers who think the idea of our characters living within dreams or illusions is nothing but a big ripoff, as if all of the fun and excitement generated by those scenes just flies right out the window once you find out that they never really happened. But if there's ever a portion of LOST that was unreal or imaginary? It was definitely the off-island events we saw when the Oceanic Six managed to escape the island.

For the better part of two seasons, these characters leave the island and live out their lives in what they perceive to be the "real world." What they could be experiencing however, is just a parallel offshoot of the island's own Limbo. This is a timeline that never should've spawned - "another life" that none of them should have ever had, and one without any sort of future. As Jack calls the freighter at the end of season three, both Locke and Ben gravely try to warn him: "You're not supposed to do this." Jack does it anyway, and from the second the O6 step off the rescue plane until the minute they board Ajira 316 for the flight back, the entire off-island storyline has a strangely dark and mocked-up feel to it.

In an attempt to wipe away their memories of the island, the Oceanic Six all decide to stick to one big gigantic lie. Hurley is the only person to protest. "But what if we all do?" Hugo suggests, of telling the truth. "If we can stick together, we can make them believe us." Hurley's idea is shot down quickly, and the exact opposite happens: everyone sticks together, but with lying about the plane crash instead. This one big deception becomes the focal point for the entire off-island timeline - a timeline that exists for only as long as the Oceanic Six keep lying about it... not so much to the public, but to themselves.

Take a good look at the off-island world for a moment, and you'll realize it looks just a little *too* good. Each member of the O6 starts off with a flawlessly clean slate of their own. Hurley gets welcomed back to a happy family, and is reunited with the father who left him. Sayid meets up with and marries the love of his life, Nadia. Kate gets away with murder, settles into a beautiful house, and falls happily into motherhood with little Aaron. Sun safely gives birth to Jin's baby, Ji Yeon. And not only is Jack's career back on track, but he finally gets the girl he's always wanted: Kate. Life is pretty good for everyone, with daddy issues dissolving away in an almost utopian, *Matrix*-like setting. Initially, anyway.

Slowly however, one by one, the island pulls them back. It starts with Hurley - visions of his friend Charlie driving him to realize that they never should've left. Hugo was the only one of the O6 who tried to stay pure by denouncing their lie, so he was the easiest to get to. He never fully accepted his new life, content to drive his beat up old car, throwing down a bucket of Mr. Cluck's, and eventually settling back into the security and familiarity of Santa Rosa. But even there Hugo is followed by reminders of the island: he receives visits from Abaddon, Walt and Jack, sees Charlie, and plays chess with an invisible Mr. Eko. By the time Sayid breaks into his room in the middle of the night, Hurley just shrugs and gives in. His final step in letting go occurs when he physically admits the lie to his mother, then proceeds to tell her the truth about everything that's happened on the island in one big rambling confession.

Hurley's visions are what end up corrupting Jack's perfect world. With the seeds of doubt planted, the island uses images of Christian Shephard as a crowbar to pry Jack the rest of the way open. Alcohol, drugs... as Jack spirals down, he brings Kate with him. Slowly but surely, she realizes that her perfect world is nothing but an illusion - that she'll never be permitted to just sit around playing house with her new son, who as Jack pointedly reminds her, "isn't even related" to Kate.

On the other side of the world, Sayid's own utopia is shattered in an instant by the death of Nadia. We learn during *The Incident* that perhaps Jacob even had a hand in what happened. If he wasn't directly responsible for Nadia getting killed at that intersection, he almost certainly could've prevented it. Yet he didn't, and that's likely because Jacob is the one trying to get the Oceanic Six back to the island. Just as his nemesis worked so hard to get them off, Jacob's next move is to bring them back, so they can continue on with the storyline as it *should* have occurred.

Seeing The Truth... Behind All The Lies

Even with the help of Benjamin Linus and Ms. Hawking, none of the Oceanic Six can return to the island until one very big prerequisite is met: they dissolve their own lie. Once again belief and faith come into play here, because the off-island world in which the characters now exist is a fabrication they created all on their own. Until they unravel it themselves - once again cleaning up their own mess - each person is trapped within his or her own invention. Ben tries to explain this to Hurley during *The Lie*, telling him: "Come with us, Hugo... and this will be over. You can stop hiding. You can stop worrying about the stories and the deceptions. If you come with me, you won't ever have to lie again."

For Jack, it takes seeing his walking dead father and hearing Charlie's message to realize his error. "I'm sick of lying. We made a mistake", he tells Kate, in LOST's ultra-dramatic, first-ever flash-forward. "We were not supposed to leave." The representation of this idea doesn't end here, either. It goes one step further when Hurley flat out tells Jack, as well as us, that the Oceanic Six "never left that island" at all.

Sayid's big lie includes becoming a trained killer and assassin, nudged into this role by Benjamin Linus. "I'm not what you think I am", he first tells Ben. "I don't like killing." This concept is backed up by Nadia's own words in the season one episode, *Solitary*. When Sayid was willing to sacrifice his job as a communications officer for promotion to torturer, he assures her "This isn't a game, Nadia." "Yet you keep playing it", she tells him, "Pretending to be something you're not."

Throughout his entire off-island existence, Sayid continues pretending - mercilessly killing anyone Ben tells him to. Ultimately it takes his affair with Elsa in *The Economist* to finally realize his lie. After being shot, Sayid lies on the bed watching Elsa in the full length mirror. She is a killer pretending to be someone else, a total reflection of himself. In fact, just as he breaks the mirror Sayid sees actually himself in the reflection instead of Elsa (go back and watch that part, it's pretty cool). By shattering the mirror he symbolically puts an end to his career as a murderous assassin, taking up a hammer and nails to help the needy in Santo Domingo.

Sun's only lie was telling the public that her husband, and everyone else on Flight 815, had died in the crash. Upon seeing Ben produce Jin's wedding ring, she's quickly ready to go back to the island. This leaves Kate and Aaron as the last of the Oceanic Six still secure in the realm of the off-island world, and Kate resists up until the very end. Knowing that triggering Kate's flight instinct is the surest way to jolt her into leaving that comfort zone, Ben arranges pressure in the form of lawyers looking to take custody of Aaron. The fear of losing her son, coupled with her maternal instincts to do the best thing for him, causes Kate to finally see through her own lie. In fact, her lie just might be the biggest lie of all, because...

Aaron Never Existed Within the 06 Timeline

When you examine the sum total of the flash-forwards

within seasons four and five of LOST, there are lots of times when things just don't seem real. From Jack and Kate's fantasy game of house to Sayid's super-spy assassin plotline, things often fall outside the realm of believability. Take Aaron's refrigerator artwork miraculously showing up on the walls of Santa Rosa... or Jack twice mentioning his father as if he were still alive. There are aspects of this timeline that are bizarre and strange, and others that are just plain 'off'. At one point Hurley even mocks Jack's belief that everything's fine: "Living with Kate... taking care of Aaron... it all seems so perfect... just like heaven." Jack responds by defending reality itself. "Just because I'm happy doesn't mean that this isn't real" he tells his friend, to which Hurley wistfully responds "I was happy too Jack... for a while, anyway."

Happiness... complacency... these are the building blocks of any good fantasy world, and the Oceanic Six started off strong. But as the curtain of deception is finally raised on their rapidly crumbling lie, one of its biggest illusions is uncovered: Aaron may have never actually left the island at all.

If Claire's infant son is a part of the off-island illusion experienced by our characters, then Aaron was undoubtedly perpetuated by Kate. Jack had his job to get back to, Hurley had his family, Sun had Ji Yeon, and Sayid would have Nadia. Back in the "real" world, Kate was the one character who had absolutely no one. Aaron would become the one reason Kate would have for continuing on, despite facing a life behind bars. As Cassidy would later tell her during *Whatever Happened,*

Happened, "You needed him." Miraculously and once again unbelievably, Kate is spared any prison time at all, being allowed to not only keep Aaron but to raise him as her own. In her perfect, happy little fantasy, Kate gets to play the role of mom, homemaker, and even the future Mrs. Shephard.

Along the way however, there are some fairly big clues pointing to the fact that Aaron's not really there, and sometimes they're even hidden in plain sight. The first is during the Oceanic press conference, where Kate is holding Aaron, arms folded over him protectively. Every one of the Oceanic Six have name tags set in front of them, except for the baby. And even as one reporter asks about Aaron's name and age, he looks directly at Kate without even glancing down at her child.

In *Eggtown*, Kate's lawyer Duncan wants desperately for her to bring someone into the courtroom. "We need him, Kate", he pleads with her, "It will generate tremendous sympathy." Kate refuses on the simple grounds that she won't "use her son", keeping the judge, jury, courtroom, and even the lawyers from ever laying eyes on Aaron. But if you watch this scene again carefully, Duncan never mentions Aaron at all. Because of Kate's reaction, we just assume that's who he meant. There's a good chance Duncan wasn't referring to Aaron, but to Jack instead - a surprise witness he winds up calling later on to generate sympathy for Kate's case. Rewind to when Kate gets remanded into custody as a flight risk, and Duncan's protest doesn't include Aaron there either. The fact that she's the baby's only surviving parent might've helped her make bail, but it wasn't even mentioned.

The next person who wants to see Aaron is Kate's mother Diane. After telling Kate that she no longer wants to testify against her, Diane says "I want to see my grandson. I just want to *see him*." Kate once again refuses, this time vehemently: "I don't want you anywhere near him. We're finished!" It's as if Kate knows on some level that Aaron isn't real, and is keeping him from everyone else to protect her own tenuous illusions of motherhood.

As the two lawyers argue over whether or not Kate will spend jail time, they talk about everything from her heroics during the plane crash to Kate rescuing her mother from an abusive husband. The one thing they don't mention however, is Aaron himself. "I have a child", Kate states firmly, as if reminding herself of this fact as much as she's reminding them. "I'm not going anywhere."

Cue Jack, who ambushes Kate in the parking garage to score a date. She invites him over, but it's clear Jack hasn't been to Kate's house yet, and hasn't seen Aaron since their rescue. When he suggests coffee instead, Kate gets somewhat angry. "I know why you don't want to see the baby, Jack", she tells him. "But until you do...until you want to, there's no you and me going for coffee." Kate's choice of words can be taken quite literally here... Jack must *want* to see the baby in order to see him, because until he does, he's showing up at a big old house with an empty nursery.

Later on we see that Jack not only accepts Aaron, but he actually embraces a paternal role in his life. Wanting very badly to make his romance with Kate work could be what enables Jack to finally see the baby. The three of them move in together, and Jack ends up reading Aaron bedtime stories from *Alice in Wonderland* during *Something Nice Back Home*. "I love seeing you with him", Kate tells Jack. "I'm so glad you changed your mind." The *Alice* references continue with the poster of a white rabbit hung on Aaron's door - one that conveniently disappears as the O6 storyline draws to a close.

But if the fabric of this off-island reality is dependant upon faith and belief, perhaps Aaron becomes only as real as people like Jack and Kate make him. Perception plays an important role here, as it does all throughout LOST. At the funeral of Jack's father, Kate's holding Aaron when Carole Littleton approaches her. It's just them, and no one else is around - we're seeing this scene through Kate's own eyes, without another single person in frame. "Your son is beautiful", Carole tells her, and this is exactly what Kate wants and needs to hear. But later on during *The Little Prince*, Carole wouldn't even remember Kate's baby when Jack mentions him. "Who's Aaron?" she asks, after Jack tries to explain his actions. "I.. I'm not following you." One minute later Jack's back in the car with Kate, telling her the literal truth: "She doesn't even know that Aaron exists."

The very core of this theory boils down to one thing: Aaron's existence is directly proportional to Kate's need for him. In the beginning everyone can see him - Hurley, Nadia, Sayid, Cassidy... but as each of the Oceanic Six's off-island lies start to unravel, Aaron becomes less and less visible. The biggest evidence of all comes during *Whatever Happened, Happened*, in the scene where Kate stops at the supermarket. She asks a stock boy where the juice boxes are, gets distracted by Jack's call, and that's when Aaron flat out disappears. Watch the look the stock boy gives her when Kate tells him she's lost her son: as he says "excuse me?" his facial expressions register confusion, not concern for someone who just walked by with a little blonde boy in tow. Rewind to when Kate first asks the question, and the stock boy never even looks at Aaron. In fact, no one looks at Aaron in the supermarket at all, except for Kate.

As Kate frantically runs through the aisles the next scene is shown, not surprisingly, in the store's giant wall mirror. As in Sayid's case, this is a physical reflection of her own lie: Kate is not Aaron's mother and she shouldn't be raising him. Suddenly she sees Aaron again, this time being led away by what looks to be Claire. We know from season one that Claire is *supposed* to raise Aaron, and the island is showing her this. It's slapping Kate in the face with some hard reality: since the moment they left the island, she's been deceiving herself.

This leads Kate back to Cassidy's house, where she cries: "I don't know what happened. We were in the supermarket, and I turned around for one second, and he was gone." As Cassidy consoles her, Kate goes on to say "The crazy thing is... is that...

as scared as I was... I wasn't surprised. All I could think was, it's about time." Cassidy tells Kate she feels this way because she herself took Aaron. "I had to take him", Kate argues, "he needed me." And that's when Cassidy's words strike straight to the truth of the matter: "You needed *him*." Her assertion is a more accurate evaluation of the situation: Kate needed Aaron, instead of the other way around. The very second Kate began wondering if Aaron wouldn't be better off without her? He suddenly and instantaneously disappeared.

Kate is the last of the O6 to give up her lie, and this means letting go of her son. In one of the final scenes of *Whatever Happened, Happened*, Kate relinquishes custody and hands Carole a picture of Aaron on a tire swing. Glancing down at the photo, Carole immediately asks "Where is he?" Kate answers her question with "two doors down", but Carole continues to stare at the picture. Does she see her grandson? Probably not. We've already experienced an identical situation during *Dave*: the idea of one person seeing something within a photo that's not really there to begin with. Once Kate leaves, it's likely that Carole is going to be equally disappointed when she opens the door to an empty hotel room.

So at what point does Aaron disappear? Although Kate assumes responsibility for him while still on the island, this suspiciously happens just after ghost Christian Shephard leaves Aaron lying comfortably on a bed of palm fronds. Did he pull the old baby switcheroo? Is the real Aaron still with Claire? As Christian tells Locke an episode later, "The baby's where he's supposed to be."

Exactly what happened to Aaron is pretty mysterious, because he's clearly part of the O6 rescue. Sun helps get him on the chopper, and Penny hands him off with a "goodbye sweetheart" just before the Oceanic Six float over to Membata. So does Aaron evaporate the moment they land in Hawaii? What gives?

This is a tough call, because if you remember correctly Aaron wasn't supposed to be born at all. He even stops moving after the crash, causing Claire worry and concern. It's not until Jin feeds Claire that the baby begins kicking again, perhaps the first signs of life in a very LOST place where new life is not supposed to exist. Kate helps deliver him, Charlie helps raise him, Eko baptizes him, Sun babysits him... in a way Aaron belongs to all of the Flight 815 survivors, both on and off the island. His very existence could be tied to the sum of their own beliefs. Aaron's the one good thing to come out of a really bad situation, brought into the island's universe at the exact moment Boone leaves.

Examining the theory of whether or not Aaron is real could be a huge clue as to how LOST works - maybe even the key to unlocking the entire show. Whenever faith is questioned we always seem to witness immediate consequences, and this might be for a very fundamental reason: belief equals reality.

Before letting the supermarket scene go, I want you to watch it one more time. During the chaos of losing Aaron, Kate runs past several of the aisles. Look carefully and you'll see that she passes the same woman twice... but in two different places, and wearing *two different outfits*. It's almost like watching an old Scooby-Doo cartoon, where he and Shaggy are running through a haunted house and passing the same set of cobwebs over and over again. Eventually, even as a kid, you realize that the background is *looped*. It's *not real*. Move the characters slowly and you'd never notice it, but move them quick enough and you can finally see the deception for what it really is. Kate's moving so quickly here - and her faith fading so rapidly - that maybe the island can't keep up the illusion of what's going on. Maybe the island slips up... but Kate's too fixated on Aaron to notice it.

When it comes to LOST, you should never stop trying to see beyond the curtain.

LOST -
One Big Repeating Loop

"Call me a broken record."
- Jack, *The Moth*

"You might catch something you missed the second time around."
- Locke, *Eggtown*

"History is about to repeat itself. Right here, right now."
- Benjamin Linus, *Through The Looking Glass*

"Loop dude, loop."
- Hurley, *Lockdown*

Even before the concept of time travel was officially introduced on LOST, there were subtle and not-so-subtle hints that the characters weren't always doing things for the first time. Those hints came in the form of repeated scenes, role reversals, flashbacks, and especially the dialogue. Over and over we watched the same scenarios unfold, sometimes in different places or with different characters, but many times in precisely the same way and with the same set of results.

If LOST doesn't contain some sort of temporal loop, how else can you explain Jack waking up twice in the jungle, splayed out in the exact same position - suit, tie, and everything - opening his eye to the bamboo forest above? And if that's not strange enough, watch the Pilot episode again and ask yourself how Jack instinctively knows in which direction to take off running. He sees Vincent, gets up, and immediately bolts full-tilt through the jungle to emerge on the beach... of all the directions he could've possibly picked, Jack somehow knows *exactly* where he's going. Sound plays no issue either - we don't hear the roar of the plane's engines or the screaming of its passengers until Jack visually sets eyes on the Flight 815 crash scene.

As Shannon says during *Whatever The Case May Be*, "There's something about this that seems so familiar." This is the case all throughout LOST, at first for the characters and then for us. Episode after episode, we're given repeat performances of scenarios we've already been presented with, and the deeper into the show we get, the more prominent these repetitions become. There are almost a dozen instances of characters waking up on their backs - from the jungles of the island to the deserts of Tunisia. Most of them begin with LOST's familiar "opening eye" zoom-out shot, showing us that the real scene begins the moment these characters wake up and begin realizing where they are.

Identical Scenes and Scenarios

We've watched Jin blown into the water during two different season finales, only to wash up on shore during two separate season premieres. Twice we've watched the smoke monster grab, crush, and drop someone shortly after reaching the island. The same monster also drags both Locke and Montand across the jungle floor in scenes that are nearly identical, pulling each of them into a dark hole leading down to the temple. We've seen two strangulations, three plane crashes, three shipwrecks, and countless numbers of chess games being played throughout LOST. Duplicates scenarios and situations are everywhere, including two different Dr. Shephards trying to work through the same severe alcohol problems.

In a show where mirrors and reflections are such a common theme, we have to wonder if coincidence really exists at all. In *The 23rd Psalm*, a very young Eko is forced to kill a man so his brother doesn't have to. In an apparent replication of this scene, Sayid kills a chicken to spare his brother the same job in *He's Our You*. Overall, this is a pretty strong coincidence. These characters having such identical experiences often creates an almost counterfeit feel to some of these scenes. But in trying to look at the bigger picture, these seemingly unrelated events impact both of these characters in the same way, creating the men they would one day become. It's also important to note that these two experiences come in the form of flashbacks, and not just the characters' on-island events. This seems to indicate that repetition isn't solely a byproduct of the island, but is enmeshed within the background stories of our heroes as well.

"It's a loop", Sayid tells us during the very first episode. In this case he's referring to Danielle's message at the radio tower, but he may as well be talking about the six seasons of LOST to follow. Characters switch roles in an ever-changing turn of events, going from captor to captive, from hunter to hunted, and from torturer to tortured. Identical scenes play out only slightly differently than ones we've seen before: Locke standing ankle-deep in the ocean after the crash of Ajira 316 parallels Jack's vision of his father, Christian, standing in the tide after the crash of Oceanic 815. Both characters stand barefoot wearing suits, and both having just come out of coffins - identical in many ways, but separated by five full seasons of the show.

In the season four finale *There's No Place Like Home*, we watch Benjamin Linus enter the frozen wheel chamber that's somehow responsible for moving the island. He falls upon entry, wounding his arm, but is still able to turn the wheel despite his injury. Not long afterward during *This Place is Death*, we see John Locke performing the same task. John also falls on his way to the wheel chamber, but this time severely injuring his leg instead. Like Ben, Locke is also able to turn the wheel, and this miraculously transports him to the same exit point Ben experiences in the Tunisian desert. The wake-up scenes are nearly identical in both cases, and they stay true to the repeating eye-opening theme we see throughout the show.

And as we get closer to the end of the story, repeating events become more and more unmistakable. When it appears that time has folded back in upon itself, some of the main characters even start questioning the believability of their own circumstances. "I've already done this once", Jack laughs mockingly in *Whatever Happened, Happened.* "I've already saved Benjamin Linus, and I did it for you, Kate. I don't need to do it again." His refusal to operate on Ben the second time around falls in line with Jack's new, post-time travel philosophy on island events: "screw it." It took five seasons of impossible coincidence and ridiculous circumstances, but it looks as if his hero complex has finally been cured.

Admittedly, some of these replicated scenes may be for storytelling purposes only. In a clever repeat of Desmond's season two morning "wake up" montage, we see the season five premiere begin with Dr. Pierre Chang going through an almost identical routine, right down to the spinning record player and early 70's music. This is a lot of fun, but it's also making light of the fact that we keep seeing the same things again and again. The show sometimes revels in giving us clues in the most obvious of places, where circumstances are so innocent it's difficult to question them.

Looped and Repeating Events

With the Flight 815 crash survivors relatively new to the island (an idea that's actually debatable in light of recent events), some of the bigger clues about looping come from The Others. Ben's people have been there longer than anyone save Richard Alpert, indigenous guardians of whatever secrets they might be keeping. The fact that they speak Latin is a big indication of how long The Others have existed on the island. And up until the recent fertility problem, the gauntlet of power had been handed down from generation to generation, following a strict testing process used to choose their new leader. As we see during *Cabin Fever*, as Richard tests a younger version of John Locke, the test itself involves the new leader inherently knowing which of several strange items "already belong" to them.

This suggests some sort of loop. If not a time loop, it's at least a loop of consciousness or being. Richard is checking to see that young John has recollection of events he somehow has yet to experience. Reincarnation comes to mind here; the idea that Locke would have memories of a previous life as leader on the island. LOST's storyline is thick with these references to resurrection and reincarnation. We've seen many people brought back to life on the island, most of them by our main characters (at least a half-dozen people have been saved through CPR alone), and in John's case, perhaps even by Jacob himself. The ghosts of dead characters have walked and talked; this happens within the flashbacks, in the outside world, and even through mediums such as Miles Straume. At this point we're not even sure what dead means anymore, having seen the return of so many characters in one form or another. Ben's assertion that "dead is dead" is not something that should be easily trusted.

"This is not the first time we've done this, John", Ben tells Locke during *The Brig*. These words not only apply to the activities of Ben's people, but to all of LOST in general. The island itself supports the loop motif when it shows Locke a repeating vision of Horace chopping trees to build his cabin. Over and over the same ghostly clip is played: a tree is felled, Horace says a few words, and the island rewinds the scene back to a moment where the tree is standing upright. It's a splice of time cut from the past, much the same way the Swan orientation film had a piece cut out of it. This small looped movie reinforces a circular theme, shown to John by the island in order to usher him toward his next goal.

Later on in LOST's story, some of the main characters are thrown backward through time, forced to live out their current lives within the realm of the island's past. Yet long before this happens, we get certain clues that some of our heroes are experiencing their own internal versions of Deja Vu. We can't say for sure that they're encountering the same situations, because as viewers this is our first time through the story. But at the same time, actions and dialogue don't always fit people going through these experiences for the first time. In many cases, there's evidence of reiteration... and even the characters are confused about it.

For example, take the season one episode *All The Best Cowboys Have Daddy Issues*. When Hurley tells Jack that Ethan isn't on the Flight 815 manifest, Jack immediately asks the question "Where's Charlie?" At this point there's no reason for Jack to suspect that Charlie's in danger, yet it's his first and only question. He takes off running the very second Locke tells him that Charlie went after Claire. It's almost as if Jack *knows* what's about to happen to his friend, and is trying to prevent it. He encounters Ethan alone in the jungle, receives one final warning to stop his pursuit, and then Jack is kicked in the face and loses consciousness. When he comes to, Jack sees Kate. Venomously, he tells her: "I'm not letting him do this." Kate questions Jack with the phrase "Not letting him?" to which Jack responds strangely "Not *again*."

It's the 'again' part that's troubling here. Shortly afterward, Jack and Kate come upon Charlie hanging half-dead from some trees. An earlier theory has already explored the possibility that perhaps Charlie died here, and it was Jack's faith and belief that somehow brought him back. This begs the question: Did Jack's extended effort stem from the fact that Charlie died here once before? It's clear during this very powerful scene that Jack emotionally *needed* to save his friend. If this is the second time Jack's been through this situation, perhaps he went through the pain of watching his friend die the first time around. Maybe on some level, he somehow even remembers it.

Jack's sudden clarity could be attributed to him being unconscious a few minutes earlier after fighting with Ethan. Semi-consciousness has always brought us answers on LOST, and so has near-death experience. In fact, when a very dazed Charlie finally does start talking again, he says: "Claire... that's all they wanted." These are some of his first words. "They?" Jack questions him, looking puzzled. "All they wanted was Claire", Charlie confirms again. The strange part is that at this point, "they" don't exist yet. We have no idea that anyone other than a single person, Ethan, has been working against the Oceanic 815 survivors.

Do I Know You?

As the show's characters encounter one another for the first time, there are dozens of occurrences where they seem to recognize each other. "Who are you?" isn't so much an outward question as it is an internal search for remembrance. In some cases there are reasons the characters would remember each other, such as Desmond's recollection of meeting Jack at the stadium. But in others, the kinship between strangers seems an almost intangible connection.

Take Desmond encountering Charlie on the streets of London during *Flashes Before Your Eyes*. "Where do I know you from?", he asks, as his on-island memories begin coming back to him. But to this particular version of Charlie,

Desmond is unrecognizable. Charlie takes him as a lunatic because he doesn't honestly know him... yet, anyway.

Sometimes the familiarity between characters is instinctual. Watch Kate give in to Sawyer while attempting to get Shannon's asthma inhalers during *Confidence Man*. Their initial kiss turns passionate - it suddenly seems familiar to them, like they've done it before. It's almost as if they *remember* it. And when Kate tackles Sawyer in *White Rabbit*, he playfully says "Well it's about time! I made this birthday wish *four years ago*." The statement itself doesn't seem to make any sense. Four years ago from when? What exactly does that mean?

Jump ahead to the beginning of season three, where Jack meets Juliet for the first time. He asks about the station The Others have imprisoned him in, and also about the Dharma Initiative. "They called it the Hydra", Juliet tells him. "So you people are just whatever's left over of them?" Jack asks, matter-of-factly. Juliet's response is sullen. "Well, that was a long time ago", she responds, looking very contemplative. After glancing downward for a few seconds, she adds "It doesn't matter who we were. It only matters who we are."

Could it be that Juliet somehow, on some subconscious level, remembers her three years in 1970's Dharma? At this point she wouldn't - Juliet came from the mainland, long after the Dharma Initiative had been wiped from the island. Yet her reaction here is strange, and her words to Jack don't deny being part of Dharma at all. Later on, when she sees Sawyer for the first time, Juliet smiles at him and tosses him a canteen. To say she remembers her future lover here would be a pretty long stretch, but it's interesting that in this scene Juliet becomes the first person to call him "James."

Early Foreshadowing

If you think for one minute that LOST's writers and producers hadn't mapped out the story's bigger twists and turns from the very beginning, think again. Rewatching the show, you can go all the way back to season one and find some very concrete examples of foreshadowing. Events, scenes, and even character deaths are foretold, many times through sarcastic "throwaway" dialogue that we, as viewers, don't always pay much attention to.

In *Whatever The Case May Be*, Michael is arguing Sawyer's ability to open the marshal's case. "If you pick the lock on a Halliburton, I'll put you on my back and fly us to LA", Michael tells him. Sawyer replies by quipping: "You better find yourself a runway daddy, cuz there ain't a lock I can't pick." Ironically enough not only *is* there a runway, but Sawyer will actually be building it two seasons later.

"What if a shark attacks?" Walt asks his father during *The Greater Good*, concerned about their upcoming escape from the island. "A shark's not getting anywhere near us", Michael tells him. One season later, both Michael and Sawyer are harassed by a shark as they float on the broken wreckage of their raft. In the same episode, Charlie's death is foreshadowed when he gets the "Itsy Bitsy Spider" nursery rhyme ominously wrong. Instead of "washed" the spider out, Charlie uses the word "drowned." His mistake doesn't go unnoticed either, because Hurley corrects him. At the end of season three, Charlie is killed by drowning.

We see more foreshadowing in *The Moth*, as Sawyer is jealously comparing his leadership abilities to Jack's. "Hell, give me a couple of band aids, a bottle of peroxide, *I could run this island too*", he tells Kate. At this point we have no way of knowing that Sawyer would indeed end up eventually running part of the island, or at least, the security aspect of Dharma. By *Namaste* we see that Sawyer - as Jim LaFleur - has completely swapped leadership roles with Jack; suddenly he's the mature, responsible one in charge of everyone's safety, while Jack takes on Sawyer's old carefree attitude. He goes on to tell Kate "The difference between us ain't that big, sweetheart", and in many ways, Sawyer is proven to be right.

These are more hints of predetermination than anything else. Foreshadowing is a plot device used in the telling of many stories, and LOST is just one example. At the same time however, the recurring themes within the show keep presenting themselves in a very repeating, loop-like fashion. The Flight 815 survivors even build their raft twice, after Walt burns it down the first time around. "We learned a few things from building the first one which is saving us from trial and error", Michael tells Jack. "Now it's just trial." These exact words are echoed strongly in Jacob's conversation with his gray-haired enemy: "It only ends once. Anything that happens before that is just progress."

If LOST's story is revealed to be a repeating loop, perhaps there's some type of progression that gets made each time through. The dark-shirted man doesn't see it this way, but it looks like Jacob does. He plays the optimist, believing that the end goal can eventually be reached. His nemesis is the pessimist, tired of playing, always looking for a way out. His very choice of words, "loophole", seem to indicate that he's sick of watching the same events unfold, again and again, with same eternally disappointing results.

Time Loops and Time Travel

Since the show's inception people guessed at it, but it wasn't until Desmond was catapulted back into his own past that we were slapped in the face with the idea of time travel on LOST. *Flashes Before Your Eyes* forever changed the way we'd look at the show: instead of only worrying about what was going to happen next, we now also had to worry about what *might have already happened*. The idea was crazy, kooky, scary and cool - all at the same time. And while many fans had a hard time wrapping their heads around the initial concept, the way LOST has managed to pull it off so far has more than fulfilled the expectations of even the most hardcore critics of the idea.

"There is no loop", Jack tells Hurley in the middle of season two. By this time, Jack's record is not unblemished; he's been wrong about a good many things. His inability to adapt to the island's flow and ideologies seems to be eroding away his control, and Benjamin Linus ends up getting the best of Jack in numerous ways before capturing him during the finale. Hurley doesn't believe Jack here, telling him "Loop dude, loop." In this case Hugo is making reference to Jack knowing things that he does not, but overall the metaphor is as strong as ever. During *Solitary* Hurley calls for a "do over", and in that same scene Charlie chimes in by educating him on the use of the term "mulligan."

If the progression of LOST's story could be compared to drawing a giant circle, the ending would meet back up at the beginning. With six full seasons of story to be told, the halfway or 180-degree mark would be just after the season three finale. The season four premiere would mark the point where the story arc begins climbing back toward its origins, which may be why that episode is called *The Beginning of The End*. For a long time viewers of the show have speculated that the show might, through some sort of loop, revisit the original crash of Flight 815 - a moment that's now sacrosanct amongst the cult following of LOST's diehard fans.

The idea of time travel presents an easy mechanism for such a loop to occur. Ben's turning of the frozen donkey wheel flings the island back through time, but also throws the wheel off its axis. As Daniel Faraday explains, it's like being on a record that's "skipping." Eventually a second turning of the wheel by John Locke corrects this problem, setting the needle of the island's record player back down securely in the year 1974. Many of our main characters go along for the ride, being forced to relive a time in the island's history where Dharma and The Others were locked in a deadly struggle for control.

Had nothing else happened, it could be argued that Sawyer, Juliet, Jin, Daniel and Miles would've lived out the 1970's, 80's and 90's on the island. Time would flow continuously and unbroken, up to the point where Flight 815 makes its crash landing on the island in 2004. At this point events would unfold to motivate Ben to turn the wheel once more, causing the time loop to happen again... and again... and again. The repeating circle of events between 74' and 04' would continue ever onward, occurring over and over, unless something happened to break the cycle.

We know now that it didn't happen this way... or at least it looks like it didn't. One major paradox resulting from such a scenario would be the creation of duplicates. The aforementioned characters would already exist on the island by the time Flight 815 arrives, creating a scenario where there would be two of each of them. To explain this, it could be argued that course correction does something to eradicate or kill these characters off before the crash occurs, preventing that paradox. Since we've already seen the death of Charlotte, we know that people can certainly die in the past. In that case, whatever happened would still have happened. If Juliet was successful in setting off Jughead's nuclear core, maybe these characters (Jack, Kate, Hurley and Sayid included) were all killed or wiped out at that exact moment.

This however, leaves other problems. Because from what we know of the 2004 timeline, Radzinsky and Dr. Chang survive that blast long enough to both build the Swan hatch and make several Dharma orientation tapes in the 1980's. This leaves the possibility that something *different* happens when the bomb goes off. It may be something never before seen in all the repeating loops - a new set of events, or possibly even a new timeline. Just as the dark-shirted man had a loophole that he used to kill Jacob, this new set of events could be Jacob's own special loophole. This may even be what he means by his dying words: "They're coming."

Whether the bomb goes off or not, we've already seen loops within LOST that fold back in upon each other. In *The Little Prince*, Sawyer watches the past replay itself in the form of Aaron being born on the island. Crouched in the bushes, he watches Kate deliver the baby exactly as she does in season one. So was Sawyer always there, even the first time around, when we were initially shown that scene? Or is this a new sequence of events that causes Sawyer to go back and witness this scenario for the first time? In the same episode, on the same night, Locke watches the beam of light emanating from the hatch door. Rather than interfere with the season one version of himself, Locke chooses to remain quietly in the jungle. "You could tell yourself to do things different",

Sawyer suggests to him. "Save yourself a world of pain." Locke shakes his head in disagreement. "No," he says in response. "I needed that pain to get to where I am now."

The paradox created by the same people existing in the same timeline occurs in both instances mentioned above, but it's not until *Follow The Leader* that we actually *see* two people in the same spot. As Locke and Ben watch from the jungle, Richard patches up an earlier version of John's wounded leg. That version of John Locke flashes away during the period that the island is still skipping through time, but for a brief few moments, there were two of the same person within yards of each other. This seems an impossibility given the circumstances, but it happens nonetheless.

The Point of No Return

A circle really doesn't have a beginning or an end. When you're dealing with time however, there has to be a moment when everything rewinds back to its point of origin. Rolling with the idea that all of our Flight 815 survivors are stuck in a time loop, the moment of reset occurs when the frozen donkey wheel gets turned. In 2004 the timeline reaches the end, and the last song is played. The arm of the record player rises, swings around, and resets to its initial position... where it then starts playing the first song again: 1974 Dharma.

But from the second our heroes arrive on the island until the moment Ben spins the reset wheel, it's clear that The Others are trying to accomplish some sort of goal. All of Ben's efforts seem geared toward making something important happen, from the building of the runway on Hydra island to the identification and listing of which characters are critical to his overall strategy. Whatever he's trying to accomplish, all of his plans fly out the window when the terminal event occurs. At this point success becomes impossible. This is the moment of failure, the instant after which Ben's (and perhaps even the island's) final objective can no longer be achieved in the current timeline. If we had to pick a likely spot where this occurs, it's probably the exact moment that Jack calls the freighter to the island.

"I'm telling you this because history is about to repeat itself", Ben tells Jack during *Through The Looking Glass*. "Right here, right now." For once, it seems as if Ben's trying to tell the truth. It's frustrating for him too, because Jack certainly doesn't believe him. All of Ben's lies and deceit have finally caught up with him, costing him any chance at credibility. With Naomi's satellite radio in hand, Jack calls the freighter despite Ben's warnings, and in defiance of Locke's sternly delivered message that he's "not supposed to do this." The freighter's arrival eventually leads to the Oceanic Six leaving the island, spawning another timeline that probably should never have happened. And while this timeline does exist, maybe whatever was *supposed* to happen can't be brought to fruition.

This is LOST's point of no return. Just as Desmond's

failure to keep pushing the button is responsible for bringing Flight 815 to the island, Jack's failure to keep the freighter away is what ultimately causes time to loop back in upon itself. The record plays on, and so does the game. Repeating events prevent any sort of substantial change, and everything remains status quo. Whatever happens, always happens. To quote Jacob's enemy: "It always ends the same."

Changing Things Up

If there is a repeating loop within LOST, how long has it been going on? Have the events on the island played out ten times already? A hundred? A thousand? Rousseau's message in the radio tower was up to seventeen million iterations, but eventually even that came to an end. Along the same vein, perhaps LOST isn't doomed to an endless loop. If that's the case, chances are pretty good that we're seeing the final iteration: the one time where something important actually gets *changed*. Why make that guess? Mainly because it would make for good storytelling. It would be pretty senseless to think we're watching something that's already happened over and over again countless times, but without any hope for a resolution.

Locke says it best in *The Man Behind The Curtain*: "There's a first time for everything." As viewers, this is our first and only time through the story. But for some of the characters who've been through this before, a new and changed iteration of events takes them completely by surprise. In trying to identify where the changed timeline begins, you could easily point out the moment Desmond turns the failsafe key. As the sky above the island turns purple at the end of season two, Ben and his crew squint into the light as if not really sure what's happening. An interview with Michael Emerson conducted during the hiatus revealed a little bit more. When asked what went through his character's mind at the time, he said that Ben "wasn't surprised that they sky turned purple" but admitted that it also didn't happen "exactly as he expected."

This may be because Ben expected the Swan hatch's countdown timer to eventually reach zero, but he didn't count on what would happen when the key was turned. From here Desmond is flung temporarily back into his past, waking up in his own flat with Penny having just moved in. But this time around, Desmond somehow still maintains fleeting memories of his time on the island. Showing up to buy an engagement ring, his appearance in the store is fully expected: Ms. Hawking is there not only to meet him, but she even shows him a ring he can afford. That however, is apparently as far as the scenario was supposed to go. When Desmond says "I'll take it", Hawking is genuinely shocked and surprised. "It's perfect. I'll take it", he announces again, to which Hawking responds "No you won't!" before demanding that he hand the ring back to her. "This is wrong", she tells him. "You don't buy the ring. You have second thoughts... you walk right out that door."

This is what has *always* happened. Always until now. Hawking is confused here for a reason: Desmond is doing something new for the very first time. "You don't buy the ring, Desmond", she tells him, speaking of his future in the past tense. She then goes on to describe him breaking up with Penny, entering Widmore's sailing race, reaching the island, and ultimately pushing the button in the Swan hatch for three years. Hawking even mentions Desmond's turning of the failsafe key, revealing that she already knows every single thing that will happen to him from the moment he leaves the ring shop until the moment he loops back to return again. Only this time, things happened slightly differently. For some reason, Desmond's memories of already having done those things drives him to still want the ring. Hawking gives up in frustration and he ends up walking out of the store, ring in hand.

Although Desmond does end up ditching the engagement ring and doing all the things Ms. Hawking describes, this is the first time we get the notion that things can be changed. Destiny isn't *always* set in stone, evidenced by the look on Ms. Hawking's face in the ring shop. "I can choose whatever I want", Desmond tells her, disagreeing with her assertion that everything in his life is predetermined. This foreshadows the changes he would make once his consciousness made the journey back to the island. From here, Desmond is given jagged, disjointed glimpses into the future instead of the past. He sees things that haven't happened yet, but more importantly sees them as they're *going* to happen. If time on the island is stuck in a closed loop, The Swan implosion left Desmond with the ability to briefly see and experience small segments of it.

Desmond's biggest contribution to change is the fact that he keeps Charlie alive. Not once, not twice, but just long enough to allow the freighter to see the island. Had Charlie never flipped off the jamming equipment in the Looking Glass station, the entire second half of the show would've played out differently. Keamy and his men would never have stormed the island, and the Oceanic Six storyline would never have occurred. This alone is strong evidence that Desmond's visions aren't just random, and that they're being sent to him for a very specific purpose. Someone or something is intentionally showing Desmond how Charlie dies, so that each time he can somehow prevent it. But as Charlie survives each new attempt on his life? Forces on the island begin realigning against him, rapidly course-correcting the surrounding circumstances to put him back in death's path.

There never was any real escape for Charlie, but there was a definite purpose for Desmond's precognitive flashes. Relating this to LOST's overall battle between opposing forces, maybe even Jacob himself was responsible for wanting Charlie dead. To keep the island safe and hidden, Charlie - the only other person with the musical knowledge to play the "Good Vibrations" code sequence - had to be sacrificed. At the same time, perhaps it was Jacob's enemy who was broadcasting the warning visions that Desmond kept receiving. The dark man's countermove was to keep Charlie alive until his ultimate purpose was fulfilled, because after that, Desmond no longer had such visions.

Breaking Out of the Loop

By season five, LOST's biggest question involved whether or not anything our heroes were doing could change what happened next. It was suggested many times by multiple sources that everything we were seeing had happened before, in exactly the same way, and nothing could possibly be done to change the outcome. This eventually divided the characters into two factions: those who still believed the future could be changed or shaped, and those who had resigned themselves to the inescapability of their predetermined roles. The overall theme gained momentum as the season wore on, causing a very unique parallel situation: LOST fans everywhere began choosing up their own sides of the argument.

On one hand you had Sayid. A trusted, original cast member with a long unblemished history of kicking ass, he somehow still maintained faith that things could be changed. Quickly he hatched up a plan to kill Benjamin Linus as a child, hoping it would undo all of the evils he'd already committed as an adult. His belief that this would permanently change future events fell along the same lines as Hurley trying to rewrite *The Empire Strikes Back*. Together, these characters established the "Everything Changes" camp, and they would later be joined by Daniel Faraday, a recent magna cum laude graduate from space/time school in Ann Arbor. Faraday would sell the idea to Jack, who would push it on Kate, and together they'd drag a reluctant Sawyer and Juliet into the giant mess of *The Incident* as well. By the time the season five finale rolled around, everyone's faith and belief in the concept that circumstances could be changed was stronger than ever before... a fact that just might account for what happens next in season six.

But on the flip side of the coin you had major characters like Jack and Miles, together believing that no matter what they did or what they tried, nothing really mattered at all. At one point we watched Jack uncharacteristically lay down and give up, indifference washing over him as he mopped the floors of the Dharma schoolhouse. Miles made a very convincing pro-destiny argument in *Whatever Happened, Happened*, and Sawyer and Juliet had already started going with the island's flow three years back. Many of the same characters who were so desperately trying to be rescued in the last four seasons wound up adapting a very "if you can't beat em, join em" attitude, and understandably so. This gave rise to the "Whatever Happened, Happened" faction, born mostly out of resignation after four seasons of unsuccessfully trying to fight against the island's will.

And to top it all off you had Ms. Hawking, chief of the destiny police force, hellbent on making sure everything fell into place exactly as it was supposed to. In one of the saddest moments of season five, she sends her son Daniel to the island knowing he'd be killed by her own hand. This type of sacrifice demonstrates the stranglehold of control the island has over its own events; a mother long removed from the island's shores still gives up her only son's life to serve a yet unknown cause. But another question needs to be asked here: did she sacrifice Daniel to keep the loop intact... or was Hawking actually trying to break it?

While it's obvious from Daniel's dying words that his mother knew she would shoot him, we have to ask ourselves exactly what she was trying to accomplish. In the grand scheme of things, Faraday dying at Eloise Hawking's hand just because he's "supposed to" doesn't make a whole lot of sense. It's possible Hawking knew Daniel would eventually talk with Jack, Kate and company, trying to convince them they could change the current timeline. If she had advanced knowledge of this and wanted to keep the timeline intact, sending him back seems counterproductive and dangerous, even if she knows he ultimately dies. But if Hawking was sick of the island, sick of following orders, sick of Charles Widmore, and sick of a life filled with sacrifice? She may have sent her son to the island *because* she wants to break the endless cycle of events. Maybe she's being defiant instead of subservient. Perhaps the island pushed her to give one too many things away. Examine her words during *The Variable*, when Penny asks her if Desmond will be okay. "I don't know", Hawking tells her. "For the first time in a long time, I don't know what's going to happen next." For someone working her entire life to maintain destiny's path, an argument could be made here that perhaps Hawking's actions with Daniel actually *caused* change instead. This would explain why, after sending him back to the island, she can no longer see what the future holds.

Back to the Beginning

In the end, the circular nature of LOST may very well bring us back to its very origins: the crash of Flight 815. If so, it's pretty likely we'll see some changes this time around, as characters who've managed to survive the last five seasons may have fleeting memories of their past experiences on the island. This would be similar to the way Desmond remembers pushing the button during his second chance with Penny back in season three, realizing his mistake in leaving her and attempting to change it. It could also explain some of the more subtle mysteries associated with those first few scenes of LOST. We still don't know how Jack automatically knew which direction would take him to the beach, or why Hurley is seen holding a silver watch in one hand immediately after the crash occurs. Perhaps these things were left unexplained for a reason, cleverly inserted five years ago for one hell of a future reveal.

LOST as a Video Game or Virtual Reality Experience

"Her memory reset to the crash."
- Jack regarding Claire, *Homecoming*

"You know you don't need to die. We can bring you back next season."
- Howard Zuckerman, *Expose'*

"We're taking a time out."
- Jack, *Orientation*

"EC22 RESETTING ..... RESET COMPLETE"
- Tempest Station Computer Screen, *The Other Woman*

One of the more uncommon yet cool theories out there speculates that LOST isn't just a game being played by two sides, but that it's actually one big *video game*. At any given time the characters are acting as avatars for the person or persons playing the game, controlled by one of two different opposing sides. Our heroes can be captured, influenced, and manipulated just as many other game theories suggest, with the boundaries of the game being defined by the general rules (or Book of Laws). It's certainly an interesting idea, especially when you examine some of the game situations and motifs more closely. Strewn throughout LOST are references that could make this theory work, many of them pointing to computerized or electronic elements.

The LOST as a video game concept is explored in great detail on a very cool fan-written website called Lost is a Game (*www.lostisagame.com*). This site has been up since the middle of season two, and the webmaster has gone through great lengths to prove her ideas using many, many examples. Her overall theory suggests that the show is and always has been an electronic game. As such, the game has levels, instructions, objectives for winning... even a point system for its characters to follow.

Whether or not you believe in this theory, there are nods throughout the show to many common components we see in modern day video games. One of the biggest examples involves spawn points: places where a character would re-enter LOST's story. Over and over we've watched characters suddenly appear out of nowhere, open their eyes, and enter a scene without knowing how they got there. We obviously see Jack respawn in the same place twice, wearing near identical outfits. Locke and Ben both re-enter the story flat on their backs at a location called "the exit", thousands of miles away from where they turned the frozen donkey wheel. And as mentioned earlier in this book, both Desmond and John Locke wake up after the Swan implosion in *exactly* the same spot, looking up to *exactly* the same first-person view of the tree line as they open their eyes, in two different episodes.

You could carry the spawn point motif even further by saying the submarine dock is yet another entry point for the island. As we watched Juliet's arrival during *One of Us*, we learned that anyone traveling to the island via the submarine just magically "wakes up" in one of its bunks, having voluntarily (and conveniently) submitted to being drugged.

Either our characters are being teleported to these special entry/exit points, or they get knocked out and somehow transported there while unconscious. Realistically, both of these scenarios seem pretty unlikely. But why these exact points and positions? Why the repetition? Well if you've ever played a first-person shooter or role-playing video game, you know that there are specific places your character is forced to reappear after being killed or transported. These are called spawn points, bind points, and sometimes they go by other names, but in every game they serve pretty much the same purpose: to bring a character back into 'play' after a major event or death.

If LOST is literally a video game, this explains how the Ajira characters materialized on the island in 1974. It also explains Locke, Eko, and Desmond being respawned just outside in the jungle instead of being crushed by the implosion of the Swan hatch. It even justifies Locke and Ben respawning in the deserts of Tunisia, perhaps having just completed whatever goal they needed to move the game's plot or storyline along.

Character and Scenario Resets

Running parallel to the concept of looping is the idea of situations and characters being "reset" on the island. Just as the current timeline resets to 1974, and as Locke's vision of Horace repeatedly loops back to the beginning, many of the same situations we encounter on LOST can be explained by the island resetting certain parameters. The theatrical flipping of the countdown clock being reset every 108 minutes was a prime example of this idea. Watching Desmond at the moment he turns the failsafe key, we see many of the same elements as his life goes flashing before his eyes. This is explained perfectly at Lost is a Game: "Desmond's entire experience with the flashes was actually him experiencing his own character being reset. Think of Desmond's 'flashes' as being similar to what happened to the clock in the Swan Hatch when it would reset after the button was pushed; the numbers flashed by while it was resetting. And when the button was not pushed, the hieroglyphics flashed by."

Desmond even wakes up naked, which adds more strangeness to the situation. His reset becomes more of a rebirth, or maybe even a resurrection. Desmond should not have survived the hatch implosion, just as no one really should've survived the plane crash. Walking around placidly calling everyone "brotha!"... with his long hair and the flowing robe of a T-shirt Hurley gives him immediately afterward, there are numerous Christ references made here. The island has pushed the reset button on Desmond, and his mind is still reeling from the effects of being rebooted. And if you go back and watch the scenes immediately after Jack brings Charlie back to life? The same type of mental reset seems to have happened there too.

We saw something similar to this with Claire after she was kidnapped, but we always chalked it up to the drugs Ethan had been giving her. In *Homecoming*, she returns to camp with no memory of the on-island events at all, remembering only her life prior to the crash of Flight 815. "Her memory reset to the crash", Jack explains to a very suspicious Sayid, a character who's already having trouble believing many of the mysterious circumstances in season one. Over time however, we see Claire's memory come back in bits and pieces. As she returns to the scene of her abduction, Claire receives brief flashes of information regarding her experiences as Ethan's prisoner in the Staff medical station.

One of the most direct references to the concept of a reset occurs in the middle of season four, during *The Other Woman*. As Daniel Faraday scrambles to render the poison gas of the Tempest station inert, yet another countdown begins. With only seconds to spare before certain death, Faraday opens a valve that causes a "master caution reset" of the system. "That was a close one", he tells Charlotte and Juliet, looking down at the message on the Tempest computer's screen. And while it's possible that these words represent nothing more than an innocent display, they could just as easily have a much deeper meaning. Besides equalizing the system pressure of the Tempest's gas storage tanks, perhaps Daniel was responsible for a reset of a much different kind.

In the season five finale, *The Incident*, Sawyer again uses the term while discussing the overall situation with Kate and Juliet on the sub. "Let me get this straight", he tells them. "Jack sets off the nuke, which somehow... resets everything. So flight 815 never crashes, lands in L.A. safe and sound, and none of this ever happened." As season six finally opens, we should soon find out whether or not Jughead becomes the biggest push of LOST's reset button so far.

Multiple Lives

The concept of multiple lives is another computer game staple, and there are very few electronic games where a character will stay dead forever. We've seen many characters die on LOST, and almost as many of them have come back in some form or another. Most of them seem to be removed from the game and are somehow watching from the sidelines. It's almost like witnessing a giant game of paint ball; eliminated players are relegated to stand outside the boundaries of the paint ball field in order to watch the rest of the game unfold. And if you've ever played paint ball, you know that "dead" players are supposed to remain silent - communicating with or coaching the live players is strictly prohibited. Yet just as Ben Kenobi came back to guide Luke on to Dagobah, we've seen characters like Charlie, Boone, Libby and Ana Lucia show up beyond the proverbial grave to help our Flight 815 survivors along with little pushes and shoves in the right direction.

If LOST does have a video game element to it, perhaps we've seen evidence of multiple lives as well. Aside from the many miraculous CPR resurrections we've seen throughout the show, the characters who were "reset" to their original spawn points may have expended lives to get there. This would including everyone on board Flight 815 when it crashed, and perhaps Ajira 316 as well. Characters running out of lives are finally dead and out of the game, but those who've still got lives left are reborn or respawned somewhere else. "See you in another life" takes on yet another whole new meaning once you consider this type of theory.

Season three also provided us with one bright, shining example of multiple lives within LOST: Mikhail Bakunin. We thought he died at the sonic fence during *Par Avion*, and perhaps by this theory he even did. But a half-dozen episodes later Mikhail comes bounding out of the jungle, looking bright-eyed and bushy-tailed, and with not a single trace of the blood we last saw streaming from his ears and mouth. He didn't respawn naked as a newborn Desmond, but maybe he did respawn. His line about the sonic pylons being "not set to a lethal level" may have been nothing more than a show too, one put on for the benefit of the numerous Others circled around camp as he reported back to Ben. During their exchange, watch Mikhail's body language as he pointedly 'explains' his survival before all the Other prying eyes and ears.

Even after being shot in the chest with a spear gun, Mikhail still isn't out of lives. His willingness to sacrifice himself to stop Charlie demonstrates a true dedication to The Others' cause... or maybe he just knows he's still got a few lives up his sleeve. Either way, Mikhail is one of the cooler and more "in the know" characters when it comes to LOST. He appears to have intimate knowledge of the Flight 815 survivors and looks to be one of the more important Others on the island. Before shooting Ms. Klugh during *Enter 77*, he also makes cryptic mention (in Russian) of "another way out." This is something that's yet to be explained, and it wouldn't be all that surprising if we ended up seeing Mikhail again before season six is out.

Power, Batteries, Wiring

The issue of electrical power also seems to be a recurring theme on LOST. The cables running the Dharma stations like the one Sayid found on the beach during *Solitary* are only the beginning; there are references to wiring all through the show. Desmond crosses two wires to cause a Lockdown in the Swan hatch. Bernard searches the plane's wreckage for wires to help detonate the dynamite. Charlie steps on a trip wire during *Catch-22*, and the whole Flame Station is dramatically wired with C-4 explosive in *Enter 77*. Anthony Cooper and John Locke go dove-hunting beneath huge power line superstructures during *Deus Ex Machina*. There's even a copy of *Wired* magazine on Daniel's couch when Widmore comes over to visit him.

As if this weren't enough, batteries also become a repeating issue. Sayid needs batteries for his transmitter. Walt needs batteries for his Nintendo Game Boy. Hurley runs off to get a battery from Rousseau, and Michael uses liquid nitrogen to freeze the battery keeping the freighter from blowing up. Jack also pulls the battery out of a beeping smoke detector during his flashback in *Something Nice Back Home*, symbolic perhaps of not only severing some degree of electronic ties, but also of severing his connection to the off-island world of the Oceanic Six. And in an already mentioned scene, the batteries for Hurley's walkman run out dead smack in the middle of a very cozy musical montage at the end of *In Translation*. The way the montage is sharply interrupted coordinates perfectly with the exact moment the batteries die, lending to the illusion that the montage itself was being powered by Hugo's walkman.

"Where do you get electricity?" Locke asks Ben, finally putting a voice to the same question we've been asking all along. "We have two giant hamsters running in a massive wheel at our secret underground lair", Ben quips back at him. Not until season four does this question get seriously answered; Juliet finally legitimizes the power source as yet another Dharma station called The Tempest. But just how legit are we talking here? Watching the final scenes of *The Other Woman* is like watching the ending of a bad James Bond movie. Guns, gas-masks, people getting hit in the head with metal pipes... ending with a computerized doomclock counting down to zero that gets stopped with only one second left to spare? It's just a little bit too unbelievable, even for LOST.

Introducing giant vats of evil chemical gas in an abandoned station on the ass-end of the island made this episode bizarre and secretive from start to finish. Even after the computer system receives its reset we don't see Faraday come out of the Tempest immediately. When Kate and Jack show up, Charlotte tells them "Daniel's inside securing the facility." Jack takes her word for it, but not Kate. Having seen enough deception for one episode, she marches Charlotte back in at gunpoint to see what he's doing, and it's hard to blame her.

Computerized Instruction and References

Finding a computer on the island was a pretty big shock for us in season two, but things didn't end at the Swan hatch. Despite Dharma being gone for years, The Pearl, Flame, Hydra and Tempest stations all had working computers and monitors. Looking at each of these machines carefully however, the singular way in which our characters interact with these computers is more than a little suspicious. Even more questionable is Dr. Marvin Candle's admonishment on the Swan's orientation tape. "Do not attempt to use the computer for anything else other than entering the code", he warns Locke and Eko, after the two of them have spliced in the missing piece of the tape. "This is its only function."

For a while anyway, the Flight 815 survivors adhere to this rule. Michael is the first to break it during *What Kate Did*, when the computer terminal seems to call him over by beeping to him. Not long afterward, he's interacting with someone on the other end - a person he believes to be Walt. Instead of sharing this information with everyone else however, Michael is extremely secretive about it. It's also interesting that he's the only one to witness the communication. This was something that, at the time, had viewers questioning whether Michael wasn't just seeing what he *wanted* to see. Eventually the computer even gives him specific directions to The Others encampment.

During *Enter 77*, Locke's encounter with the Flame's computer is also for his eyes only. Amazingly (yet perhaps not surprisingly by this point), he is able to beat the chess game Mikhail has been trying for "ten years" to defeat. Once again this happens while Locke is the only one in the room, raising certain questions about what comes next. The computer then provides a short film narrated by Dr. Candle, who goes on to give Locke several options. But unlike most situations in LOST where a character is allowed to make his or her own choices, all of the initial selections John makes aren't available for various reasons. This eventually leads Locke to enter '77', whether he likes it or not.

In both cases, it's as if the Flight 815 survivors are receiving outside instruction from the computer... or from whomever's on the other end of it. In a way, this type of scenario mimics the "help" the characters receive throughout the show in the form of dreams, visions, and flashbacks geared toward educating them as to what to do next. We already know that instructions can be broadcast while sleeping or dreaming, and that should be suspicious enough. But in the case of the computers, and even the Dharma Initiative videos, people on the island are receiving information in a more direct, electronic format.

Various references to computer-based knowledge and programming also exist, scattered throughout LOST in the form of names, places, and dialogue. The Pascal Flats shown on Ben's map during *Through The Looking Glass* are a possible reference to *Pascal* - a computer programming language invented in the late 1960's (and a 9-credit waste of my college career). The word 'execute' is another commonly used programming term. Not only does it appear on the Swan's computer keyboard, but the word is also spoken during *Enter 77* as Mikhail threatens Locke with the phrase: "I'll execute you right here!" The computer term 'bug' is introduced several times also: Sayid, a communications expert, is searching for bugs during *The Greater Good*, and Jack mistakes his appendicitis for a stomach bug during *The Shape of Things to Come.* Alone these phrases might not mean so much, but if you pile them up over five seasons you can begin to see certain patterns develop.

Ethan's last name, Rom, is also a widely-known abbreviation for "Read-Only Memory." This commonly used computer term describes the memory portion reserved to load a machine's operating system, and is therefore an area of the computer that can't usually be modified. This almost makes sense when you consider Ethan's character as a whole: nearly every time we see him, he acts with a singular purpose and is unable to modify his plan. Ethan is very robotic at times, especially during season one where he attacks many of the Flight 815 survivors with what seems to be superhuman strength. The teenage Ethan we see during *Dead is Dead* is eagerly programmed - almost in a *Terminator*-like fashion - to complete his mission of killing Rousseau. And although he develops a strong bond with Claire during *Maternity Leave*, Ethan is unable to compromise his plan. Twice telling her he "wishes there was another way" around taking her unborn baby (a plan that Mr. Friendly would reveal later on to be one of Ethan's own creation), he continues onward like a juggernaut, carrying on his self-assigned agenda up until the moment Charlie finally shoots him dead.

Other Electronic Elements

One of the more visual clues to LOST's possible electronic

ties comes during *The 23rd Psalm*. Here, the black smoke monster scans Eko as if he's a giant barcode. Chattering noises accompany flashing images of his past life, floating ghostly by like small computer screens. This scene changed the way many people would view the smoke monster, bestowing an almost electronic quality to the way it operated. The same thing happens again during *Dead is Dead*, as the monster surrounds and scans Benjamin Linus with similar results.

And for an island supposedly in the middle of nowhere? There's an astonishing amount of video surveillance throughout LOST. The Swan camera feeds into the Pearl station, the Pearl feeds into the Flame, and the Hydra station has a whole array of computer monitors fixed on various positions. We've seen tracking stations, monitoring stations, listening posts... and the very impressive Dharma security room where Sawyer and Miles once worked. The sonic fence (which already seems pretty high tech for 1970's jungle living) is well-covered by cameras as well. The whole island is wired up tighter than *The Truman Show*, but that's not even the half of it. Because in all different flashbacks through all different seasons, most of our characters are constantly being watched, taped, filmed, or monitored. And let's not forget the biggest watchers of all: the voices in the jungle. If you've never read a transcript of the whispers you really should, because each one of them reads exactly like a busy online chat room.

At various moments during the show one or more characters also call a "time out", pausing the action. These usually come at critical moments where events are happening way too fast for our 815 survivors to process them. After blowing open the Swan hatch, a lot of things happen all at once. Our heroes encounter a surprise underground lair, a rapidly ticking countdown clock, and a man living down there that Jack has somehow met before. Desmond is freaking out, the computer has a bullet wound, and Kate's running through the jungle to get Sayid. "We're taking a time out", Jack tells everyone, demanding Desmond's story and then watching the Swan's orientation tape to get some idea of what's going on.

Another crazy scenario requiring a time out occurs just after the island starts flashing through time. In *Because You Left*, Sawyer shakes Faraday down for some hard answers as Daniel leads them through the ever-changing jungles of the island. "How about we call a time out so you can tell us what the hell is going on?", Sawyer tells him. And this is where Faraday is forced to finally stop and explain how their group has apparently been dislodged from time.

During *The Incident* there are actually two time outs - although the characters don't refer to them as such. The first occurs as Sawyer, Juliet, and Kate reach Rose and Bernard's beachfront bungalow. There's a definite break in the action here as Rose and Bernard try to talk them out of their continued participation in LOST's big game. But the biggest time out occurs a little bit later, just as everything within the 70's Dharma storyline is coming to an explosive head. Stopping Jack in the middle of everything, Sawyer demands that he sit down with him for five minutes. "I need five minutes, that's all", he tells Jack. "You owe me that much." Jack grants him this time out, and there's a sense of peace and quiet as they sit in the jungle to calmly discuss things - at first, anyway. Their little meeting occurs despite the fact that Radzinsky's still drilling, the security team is chasing them, and Sayid is rapidly bleeding to death in the back of Hurley's van. In any other real life situation this wouldn't make a lot of sense, but in the case of a true time out? Nothing else would be going on around them at all. Their interaction in that jungle clearing would be all that exists at the time.

Lost as a Computer-Simulated Environment

Another facet of the computer game theory involves LOST as a virtual reality experience. This incorporates many of the electronic references already mentioned above, but with less of a video game type spin to it. The overall concept explains LOST away as a form of mental vacation or adventure that takes place solely in each person's own mind, starting from the moment they stepped on Flight 815. Instead of real people with real histories and past lives, some or most of the characters in our story are just virtual avatars for those who are experiencing the realm of the island. The roles they play have been chosen by them, with the characters nothing more than preprogrammed representations. They have no real memories of their previous life - instead, trumped-up flashbacks are created only to flesh out and legitimize each character's past.

The idea is extremely similar if not identical to the movie *Total Recall*. That story's main character, Doug Quaid, voluntarily submits to a virtual reality vacation package that takes place all in his own head. After putting him under, a dream implant procedure bestows memories Quaid believes to be real: car chases, gunfights, love interests, and unbelievably radical plot lines involving all kinds of secret agent hero stuff. All throughout the movie there are references to reality, unreality, and coincidence. There's even a scene in which someone enters Quaid's dream, explains that something went wrong, and tries to talk him back to reality by getting him to take a sleeping pill. "It's a symbol of your desire to return to the real world", the Recall agent explains to Quaid. "You've got to want to return to reality. Otherwise you'll be stuck in permanent psychosis." The whole situation is nearly identical to a scene during *Dave* in which his imaginary friend tries to convince Hugo to jump off a cliff, and for exactly the same reasons. "You're still at Santa Rosa, man", Dave tells Hurley. "You never left the hospital."

Fairly close to this same idea, consider Sawyer's words to Jack all the way back in *Tabula Rasa*. "You're still not looking at the big picture, doc. You're still in civilization... I'm in the wild." Taken literally, Sawyer could be explaining that they still physically exist in the real world. But unlike Jack, who's still allowing himself to be confined by real world rules and regulations, Sawyer has mentally let go. This allows his mind to run free in the wilds of LOST's jungle playground.

Although not a fan favorite, such a theory needs to be addressed simply for the incredible magnitude of looming mysteries it can be used to explain away. LOST as a virtual world accounts for every single one of the coincidences, and for the trumped-up feel to some of the flashbacks. It accounts for the same repeating events, scenes, names and scenarios, as well as the constant reiteration of the numbers. Every fantastic event, from the smoke monster to the time travel, could all be wrapped up as part of one big exciting mind-trip package. And while I'm not a big follower of the LOST ARG's (alternate reality games), even the Ajira Airways website hints at this type of explanation: "Let us whisk you to a mystery locale - you won't know where you're going until you exit the plane into your adventure."

This would also put a whole new spin on the "Who am I?" questions our characters keep asking. Jack might not be Jack at all, but someone *playing* Jack's role across the whole island experience. The whispers become those people watching from outside of the simulation, commenting on what's happened so far. Those desiring to take themselves out of the experience are removed from the island's virtual world and wake up in the real one: people like Ana Lucia who admittedly didn't want to play anymore, or like Charlie who even sacrificed their character for the sake of others. And for some players, their ultimate goal could've been an inner enlightenment rather than just a walkabout-type adventure. Boone and Shannon are great examples of characters who've achieved some form of closure on past issues, and because of this, may have been allowed to move on earlier than everyone else.

The question then becomes not only what's real and what's not real, but who exactly is playing the game? Could you count Jack, Kate, Sawyer, and the original Flight 815 crash survivors as the only individual people wired into this virtual world? What about Benjamin Linus? Richard Alpert? The guy driving the cab that Jacob and Hurley ride in? At some point a line needs to be drawn between actual players within the game and non-player characters. If Danielle Rousseau is nothing more than part of the island's complex programming, perhaps the same could be said for The Others and their entire encampment. Or going the opposite direction, what if Jack were the only "real" person in all of LOST? What if the rest of the show turned out to be an interactive virtual experience designed around Jack's hero complex and need for control?

Like it or not, these types of theories are given definite nods throughout the show. Look around carefully, and reality has always been in question. Free will may be so important here because it's all a character really has - the entire experience may be geared toward getting these characters to face their fears and make hard choices they normally wouldn't make in their everyday lives. Change and growth come from within them, drawn out by the extraordinary circumstances they're forced to endure on the island. And in the end, this holds true whether LOST is proven to be real, fake, or otherwise.

Perception & Perspective

"I taught myself about perspective. You know what that is - perspective?"
- Michael, *Special*

"Your perception of how long your friends have been gone... it's not necessarily how long they've actually been gone."
- Daniel Faraday, *The Constant*

"That is not what I saw."
- Mr. Eko, *The Cost of Living*

"It's all in the details... and they're wrong."
- Sawyer, *The Long Con*

In this book you've read theories on just about everything. Hopefully by now, you've even developed some of your own. In that respect, LOST isn't like most television shows - it's a unique and one-of-a-kind experience. The show's true appeal lies in the way events can often be interpreted differently from one viewer to the next, and by the end of an episode, each individual usually has his or her own take on what just happened.

This makes LOST a perspective-based experience. As we watch it, what you see and what I see might be two totally different things. This last theory picks up on the very same concept, because if you take the time to stop, step back, and look at LOST's bigger picture? You'll realize that what's happening on the show at any given moment isn't always as important as *who* it's happening to.

Let's start with the scene in *Numbers* where Locke's building what looks to be an animal trap. Claire's watching him the whole time, and she even helps build it. Up until that moment, Claire has seen Locke very one-dimensionally. To her, John Locke has been little more than a jungle-stalking, knife-wielding hunter. But the moment he turns the trap over, it suddenly becomes a cradle. Her perspective has changed. The object they built stayed exactly as it always was, but Claire is now looking at it from a different angle, just as she looks at John differently from that moment on.

This type of mirror-image duplicity is what makes LOST such a fantastic puzzle. Sometimes the answers are right in front of our faces all along, but we can't see them because we're not looking at them correctly. Every once in a while, the writers and storytellers will flip a piece of that puzzle over, or turn it in a different direction, and suddenly we can *see* the answer. But just as Claire never knew she was looking at her baby's cradle the whole time, there are many occasions on the show when we're looking right at something and not seeing it for what it truly is.

This is especially true of LOST's main characters. Perspective is such an important part of the show that many of its most critical opening shots start off with an extreme close-up of someone's eye. This is more than just a clever camera angle, this is a tremendous clue as to what's going on. Because when you're seeing that eye, most of what you'll be viewing that episode is through the eyes of the character it belongs to. Everything that happens, happens the way *they* see it. Jack-centric episodes are based upon Jack's interpretation of what's going on. Locke-centric scenes are showing us the world through his eyes. Over and over we've seen the story being told from outside, third-person camera angles... but at the same time, we need to realize we're also watching an interpreted version of events. What you see isn't always what you get.

Everything Changes

We get our first real taste of this philosophy as the 815 survivors blow their way into the Swan hatch to encounter Desmond in early season two. The first three episodes showed the action from three different perspectives, and each of them was slightly different. What Jack saw during *Man of Science, Man of Faith* wasn't exactly the way Locke saw things go down during *Adrift*. An episode later, we see Kate's perspective of the same hostage situation unfold as she crawls through the air ducts during *Orientation*. The scene was obviously shot more than once for effect, but a good many things are different. The way Desmond holds the gun to Locke's head varies from episode to episode, and the dialogue is inconsistent too. Jack and Locke hear Desmond's now legendary first use of the word "brotha!", but in Kate's view of that scene the word is oddly omitted.

Such small differences can be easily chalked up to having shot the scene multiple times, but this is only the tip of the iceberg. In Desmond's exercise sequence that opens episode one, everything in the hatch looks a certain way. Yet once Jack, Locke, and Kate enter the picture, many aspects of the hatch decor look suddenly different. Lamps and tables have changed. The record player is a whole different model, and the record collection is arranged differently. Even the mural switches up a bit. These changes were so radical that fans picked up on them almost immediately, spawning the debate over what could be recognized as 'clues' on LOST and what should be considered nothing more than simple continuity error.

This would be fine if Jin didn't step forward in Hurley's dream a few episodes later to tell us that "Everything is going to change." This was followed up in season three when the words "Everything Changes", flashed across the screen during the brainwashing film in *Room 23*. People watching the show began looking for subtle and even not-so-subtle changes in the scenes and scenery of LOST, and with good reason. In every season so far, important props were found to be completely inconsistent: Hurley's lottery ticket for one. Notes and lists written by Desmond, Charlie, Sayid, Ms. Hawking, and Sawyer... all of these change size, content, color and handwriting from shot to shot, sometimes even within the same episode. At quick glance they all look the same, but when held side to side with the originals? We soon see there are two or more different versions of many, many objects within LOST. This probably shouldn't be all that surprising, either. How many times have we seen two or more versions of the same person, place, or event?

Of course every one of these inconsistencies should be taken with a grain of salt; on a show as tremendous as LOST there are bound to be duplicate props and inevitable mistakes made during shooting. That being said, some of the bigger differences can't be explained away so easily. Hanging in Ben's home, we actually see two different versions of a painting we assume to be his mother. Her hair and face are clearly different from episode to episode, meaning that someone went through the trouble of painting the same portrait twice with distinct differences. And in what probably became the most infamous of all parlor tricks, the photos of Mrs. Gardner's grandson swap themselves out to all new frames - from woodgrain to metal - in the five minutes it takes Miles to Dustbust his bedroom. That kind of stuff is intentional, no matter how look at it.

For me, the big moment came during a "next week on LOST" promo for *One of Them*. They showed the Swan's countdown clock reaching zero, and the appearance of the hieroglyphs. In the promo however, the clock's numbers were black on white for the left side (minutes), and white on black for the right (seconds). In every other episode, these colors are reversed. And when *One of Them* finally aired the next week, the countdown clock looked perfectly normal again... only in the promo did they show us the reversed colors. This meant they made two props of the clock that mirrored each other perfectly, and used one of them for the sole purpose of giving us a two-second tease. And to further kick us in the ass, the clocks even had the same small dent in the lower right corner.

As Sawyer warned us during The Long Con: "It's all in the details... and they're wrong." If the details of the show can't be trusted, the next question becomes why. Why are they showing us so many different versions of things? How can the clocks on the wall skip ahead minutes and hours from shot to shot? Why do the contents of Ben's fridge completely rearrange themselves as Locke chows down on his leftovers?

Maybe the answer lies within the perspective. It might just be that each person is perceiving things differently on the island. The way Locke viewed the monster was certainly different from the way Eko saw it; two people looking at presumably the same thing, but seeing two very different results. If LOST is an ever-changing, ever-morphing environment, maybe the Swan hatch appeared the way it did in the season two opening scene because that was *Desmond's* perception of how things looked. That episode began with a shot of *his* eye opening. Once other people arrived, maybe they saw things a little bit differently. Locke even hints at this during the same episode, as he and Kate are discussing the smoke monster: "Did you see it Kate? Then I guess we're both crazy. Wonder what Jack thinks he saw?"

Perspective-Based Reality

Colors and objects change constantly throughout LOST, and in many cases there's no mistaking it. Claire's diary is black while she's holding it during the Pilot episode. Later on, after she gets kidnapped and is no longer around, her diary becomes blue. The color of Locke's compass also changes once he gives it to Sayid. Daniel's journal has an inscription from his mother that looks one way when he views it, and completely different when Eloise reads it an episode later. But the straw that breaks the camel's back occurs when Sayid drills a 12-year old Benjamin Linus straight through the heart in *He's Our You*. The very next episode Jin arrives to turn the boy over... only to find Ben shot through the *right* side of the chest instead of the left.

This is way too important to be an error in continuity. Sayid wanted Ben dead more than anything: at that point he even believed it was why he was thrust back through time. In Sayid's eyes, he saw his bullet strike exactly where he wanted and needed it to go - an assassin who knows he's fired a kill shot. After only a single bullet Sayid strides right past Ben's body and disappears into the jungle. Jin however, has no preconceived notion of where, or even if, the boy was shot. He sees the wound on the left side of the chest, and from that point on, so does Jack, Kate, Juliet and Sawyer. This enables Ben to survive long enough to be brought to The Others, where Richard Alpert goes on to save his life by taking him to the temple.

So did the island want Ben to live? It sure looks that way. If his future actions would be important to the island's sequence of events, perhaps it showed everyone what it *needed* them to see. The manipulation of perspective could be another way of controlling the characters and events on LOST without actually touching the playing pieces. In a way, it could be construed as the island's own personal loophole.

Much of LOST's imagery is perception-based. What Hurley sees as he puts his arm around his imaginary friend is not what the camera sees when his Polaroid is taken in *Dave*. And when Michael is looking at the Swan's computer during *What Kate Did*, we're seeing everything through his eyes only. No one else is around to dispute it, so we get his own interpretation of the screen. He even knocks Locke unconscious during *Three Minutes* before accessing the computer again, just so he can use it alone. Amazingly enough, the second he starts typing Walt miraculously happens to be available on the other end, giving his father exactly what he needs to see right then and there: directions to The Others encampment.

The idea behind this theory is that, in short, everything on LOST could be in the eye of the beholder. Aaron's appearance and sudden disappearance in the O6 storyline could only be scratching the surface of what's real and unreal. The very perceptions and experiences of our characters could be what's really being manipulated and shown to us - even within the flashbacks. Notice how different Christian Shephard looks when Locke encounters him during *Cabin Fever*. Unlike the cleaner visions we've seen Jack have of his father, he suddenly has very sunken features, pallid color, and disheveled hair. Maybe this is the island's raw image of Christian, taken when his embalmed corpse cartwheeled through the jungle after the crash of Flight 815. John Locke is looking at a man he's never seen before, with no preconceived idea of what he should look like. But had Jack entered the cabin, maybe his father would've looked differently - tainted by his own real-life memories of when he was alive.

So did a delirious Sawyer really scream out Wayne's message as Kate was tending to him? Did an unconscious Eko actually speak to Locke during *Further Instructions*? No one but Kate and Locke were around to see and hear those things. These questions are like asking if a tree falling alone in the forest really makes a sound - we only know what happens through Kate and Locke's singular perception of events. Had someone walked up on the Swan's computer screen while

Michael was typing to Walt, what - if anything - would they have seen?

And let's go back to Jack's interpretation of his first solo surgery, which he flashes back to during *The Incident*. Jack has talked about this scene before, all the way back in episode one. This time however, his father is there in the corner of the room, watching him. Jack doesn't "make a choice" to let the fear in for five seconds as he initially described to Kate, he panics and his father almost has to take over. Christian gets Jack to calm down by threatening to step in, and only after forcing him to do so does Jack count to five. But is Jack's father really there at all? Watching the scene again, it's difficult to tell. Again, it could be that we're getting Jack's skewed perception of events here. Nervous about his first solo procedure, it's possible that Jack simply didn't have enough faith to successfully finish the surgery on his own; he needed the vision of his father there for guidance. Later on, as Jack is angry at himself for this failure, the whole coffee-machine conversation he has with Christian might all take place in his head. Jack blames his father for not believing in him, but Christian reflects the nagging truth by asking: "Are you sure *I'm* the one who doesn't believe in you, Jack? "

Desmond's companion Donovan puts it well during *Flashes Before Your Eyes*: "Run the same test ten times, you'll get ten different outcomes." Likewise if you take the same situation seen from ten pairs of eyes, you'll get ten different versions of how things played out. Each perspective might be pretty much the same, but with small and unique differences. How things look on LOST might very depend upon who is looking at them.

The Perception of Time Travel

"There are no spaceships. There isn't any time travel." This was producer Damon Lindelof's statement in an early 2005 interview, back when LOST fans were still wildy guessing at the show's bigger picture. The inexplicable nature of the smoke monster combined with the insurmountable stack of coincidences was driving fans to assume what they perceived to be the worst possible scenario: that LOST was taking a nose-dive into the realm of (shudder!) science fiction. Either Lindelof's statement was meant to appease fans at the time, or the idea of time travel within LOST hadn't been conceived yet; on the surface, it seems like it has to be one or the other. Judging from how well-planned out the show has been - especially since it was determined that the original story arc would be allowed to be told in its entirety - it's hard to believe the latter. And although I wouldn't blame the producers one bit for fibbing about a storyline three or four seasons away, perhaps that's not the case either.

A third possibility also exists, and one that satisfies both scenarios: time travel on LOST doesn't exist at all. This may seem like a radical concept given the many crazy things we've seen in season five, but there are certain perspectives that could explain time travel in another way. In fact, we see evidence of these perspectives back in seasons three and four, even before anyone ever lays a hand on the frozen donkey wheel.

Take Desmond reliving a small snippet of his past during *Flashes Before Your Eyes*. The journey back to his former life takes place immediately after a pretty traumatic event: the implosion of the Swan. It also seems to happen within Desmond's own head, as he wakes up in the jungle only minutes or hours afterward. During *The Constant*, a similar thing occurs, only this time Desmond's trips are shorter and more frequent. We also get to see what happens to his physical on-island body as his mind takes these little jumps: Desmond passes out and goes into a sort of trance while his mind flips through the reference book of his past.

Here's a good question: did George Minkowski time travel? If you were to ask him that question, he'd sure think so. One minute he's strapped to a gurney in the freighter's sick bay, the next minute he's riding a Ferris wheel somewhere in his past life. Minkowski is mentally jumping through his own memories, but at a much faster and more dangerous pace than Desmond. Eventually it kills him, just as it kills Charlotte when she returns to the island - yet another character who travels into the realm of her own past, flipping all the way back to her childhood in the Dharma Initiative. The temporal sickness also affects Daniel's girlfriend, Theresa Spencer. We're introduced to her in *Jughead*, where we learn she's experiencing the same symptoms as the characters mentioned above. "Sometimes she wakes up, thinks she's three", her sister and caretaker Abigail tells Desmond. "Yesterday, she was talking to our dad. He died five years ago."

But if all of these jump-through-life journeys exist solely in the minds of these people, who's to say that the entire concept of time travel we see in season five isn't just an extension of this idea? If you believe that the island is skipping through time the way Faraday explains, wouldn't it be odd that only *some* of the island's inhabitants travel with it? Why do Jin and Sawyer flash away, but Danielle's science team and The Others remain unaffected? Only the characters skipping through time can see the flash of light too - they each shield their eyes when it comes, but not the people around them that they interact with. Should the island really be moving though time, what determines who goes and who stays? If Ethan and his rifle stay behind as Locke flashes away, why would Ethan's bullet still be in John's leg when he arrives at his next destination? Is the bullet there only because John's perception of events involves him getting shot?

Ready to blow your mind? Consider the possibility that *everybody* is stuck, like Theresa or Minkowski, within the realm of their own looping memories. Each person is viewing their life's experiences through their own eyes, each with their own unique perspective on how things happened. To them, they're actually living in these time periods, just as Charlotte begins talking aloud as she relives her childhood shortly before dying. If we could view that scene through her own eyes, would it appear as a flashback? To us as viewers, sure. But to her, it would be nothing more than her current timeline.

Maybe no one's traveling through time at all. It could be that everyone's just being shown an interactive history of the island, the way Locke was shown that small, repeating clip of Horace building his cabin. Just as Locke was able to speak with Horace, Sawyer and his friends would be able to interact with their own living history lesson. A wild idea for sure, but this is LOST.

Viewer-Based Reality - Believing Your Own Ears

"You can't hear everything, Boone. The sooner you learn that, the better."
- John Locke, *Special*

Alright, it's time to break out your LOST DVD's because here's where things get *really* good. Television is a two-sense medium: we can go only by what we see and hear. Already we've learned that what we see on LOST isn't necessarily what we get - at least not every time. So by the same token, trusting everything we hear would be silly as well. In watching and rewatching the show, I can point out several places where our eyes could be telling us one thing... but if we listen carefully, our ears might be telling us something entirely different.

Getting immersed in LOST can definitely put you in tuned with these types of things. In discussing the show with podcast partners Anil "The ODI" (*the-odi.blogspot.com*) and Karen (*karenslostnotebook.blogspot.com*), I quickly found that they've experienced their own little places like this in the storyline. These are moments where everything looks visually on the level, but where you just can't trust your ears. And as mentioned above, in many of these cases, the character's own perception plays a huge part in what gets said and heard within the scene.

In *Numbers*, Hurley visits Leonard Simms, playing Connect Four with himself at Santa Rosa. "Hey Lenny, remember me?", he says. "Hugo. *Hurley.*" Listen to that last word carefully. It's spoken in Jack's voice - not Hurley's. The rest of his greeting is Hugo talking, and we get a frontal view of everything he says. But that last word, "Hurley", is spoken while Hugo's back is turned to us. With a sly trick of the camera, we never get to see his lips move.

This happens again during *Tricia Tanaka Is Dead*, as Hurley chases Vincent through the jungle. "Vincent! Vincent, come here Vincent!" he shouts after the dog. But one of those three shouts you hear? It's not Hugo. Once again, this is Jack's voice. If you listen the voice change is definitely there, spoken while the camera is not trained on Hurley's face.

Skip ahead to season four, as Juliet wakes Jack up in the opening scene of *Something Nice Back Home*. "Jack... Jack? Jack!" she shouts, trying to rouse him. One of those "Jack!"'s is distinctly Kate speaking, and the difference is unmistakable. We're shown this scene from Jack's point of view too; he's semiconscious at the time and sick from appendicitis. Is this why Jack's perception of Juliet's voice is blurred? Is Kate on his mind? In this case maybe Jack's just hearing what he wants to hear, but it's interesting nonetheless.

Things however, get a lot more bizarre. Already mentioned in this book was Sayid's voice change while interrogating Henry Gale in the armory: "You want to know who I am?" This line is spoken with the camera on Sayid's back, and in this case the voice is completely unrecognizable. It's angry, malevolent, gravelly... with Ben's frightened look giving the scene an all the more spooky feel to it.

Want some even better ones? Check out the pool scene in *Do No Harm*, where Christian is talking to Jack the night before his wedding. As his son is questioning whether or not he'll succeed as a husband, Christian tells him, "Commitment is what makes you tick, Jack." Then, in some other voice that sounds suspiciously like it could be Sawyer's: "The problem is you're just not good at letting go." These last words have a definite southern twang to them. This is also the same phrase Jack would hear his father say over the broken intercom at the Hydra station. Once again, the camera conveniently pans over to Jack's face for that last part, so we never see Christian mouth these words at all.

Also interesting about this scene: Jack is dipping his feet in the water of the hotel pool, and he's half-finished with a bottle of alcohol. Being drunk or in an altered state of consciousness has traditionally had profound effects on what the show's main characters see and experience. And as rain-soaked, backwards-speaking Walt will tell you, water has always acted as some sort of catalyst on LOST when it comes to strange occurrences or plot twists. In this case you have both, and during a flashback no less.

During *The Variable*, we meet Theresa Spencer, Daniel Faraday's girlfriend. So does Ms. Hawking. As Hawking tries to ditch this girl so she can take her son to lunch, Daniel begins to protest. That's when Theresa chimes in by saying "I understand", and then, in *Charlotte's* voice instead of her own "It's okay Dan, really." This one is sneaky, because both women have a similar accent. And does the camera pan off of Theresa's face just as her voice changes over to Charlotte? You bet.

It also seems that as we get further along in LOST's story, these voice substitutions become more and more obvious. One of the biggest and best occurs during *Some Like it Hoth*, as Kate tries to comfort Roger Linus on the swing set of the Dharma barracks. Over a beer, Kate says a bit too much about young Ben's apparent abduction, prompting Roger to shake her down for answers. As she wisely flees, Kate tells him she was just trying to help. "Oh, you're trying to help, huh?" Roger asks angrily. The camera angle then changes to a shot of Kate walking away - so we don't see Roger's lips move - and that's when his next words are spoken perfectly and unmistakably in Jack's own voice: "*You wanna help, Kate?*" The voice is so crystal clear that Kate even whirls around, looking back at Roger with an astonished, uneasy look on her face. It's like

Kate *knows* what she just heard, but still doesn't believe it. "Well, why don't you just mind your own business?" Roger then finishes in his own voice, the camera back upon him as Kate picks up her pace.

A big part of LOST is about solving its mysteries. As we look for answers, we have to accept all the evidence given, even if it's not what we expect (and *especially* if it's not what we expect). Hurley's voice speaking the numbers on Montand's radio in 1988 turns out to be only a small part of the vocal trickery the storytellers of LOST have sprung upon us. Seeing the bigger picture involves looking at everything, taking it at more than face value, and trying to understand the biggest question of all: *why?* What makes our characters start hearing these voice changes, in both their on-island experiences as well as their flashbacks? And how come so many of them seem to involve LOST's most central character, Jack?

"I am Jack's complete lack of surprise."
- Narrator, *Fight Club*

An interesting version of the perception theory brings the concept of solipsism into question. Solipsism is the idea that nothing else exists except *you*. Because you think, you know that you exist. Everything else is external: the things you see, touch, interact with... the entire rest of the world, including the people and other minds within it - all of these things are unknowns. From a solipsist viewpoint, you can never be sure that anything is real at all, except yourself.

Without getting too existential, what if the sum total of LOST were nothing more than Jack's own experiences, as seen through his opening eye? From the moment that eye blinked open until the last scene of the show, is Jack's perception all that ever exists? Is this all we're being shown? Going one step further, is Jack *everyone*? Jack Shephard and John Locke could be two opposing halves of the same identity... Jack's cut from the Flight 815 crash is in the same position as the scar Locke received from his kidney being removed. Could Jack also be Jacob? His use of the phrase "He knows where to find me" during *The Other Woman* is almost identical to what Jacob tells his dark-shirted nemesis on the beach. These types of questions are fun to explore, even if there's little basis for justification.

No matter what you believe about LOST, the way the show is viewed is certainly affected by perception and perspective. This is true of the characters as well as the viewers. Long after the show ends, people will always have their own take on exactly what went down. And even though we've chased answers for so many years now? When LOST ends, maybe the most enjoyable part will include not ever *really* being sure of what we saw.